# EVERLASTING LIFE

## Kristy Phillips

WESTBOW
PRESS
A DIVISION OF THOMAS NELSON
& ZONDERVAN

Scripture taken from the Holy Bible, NEW INTERNATIONAL VERSION®.
Copyright © 1973, 1978, 1984 by Biblica, Inc. All rights reserved worldwide.
Used by permission. NEW INTERNATIONAL VERSION® and NIV® are
registered trademarks of Biblica, Inc. Use of either trademark for the offering
of goods or services requires the prior written consent of Biblica US, Inc.

Scripture taken from the *Amplified Bible*, copyright © 1954, 1958, 1962,
1964, 1965, 1987 by The Lockman Foundation. Used by permission.

Scripture taken from the King James Version of the Bible.

Book edited by:
Katelyn Williams & Josette Zielinski

Cover Image by Kristy Phillips & Dena Long
Potographer: Karina Hack

WestBow Press books may be ordered through booksellers or by contacting:

WestBow Press
A Division of Thomas Nelson & Zondervan
1663 Liberty Drive
Bloomington, IN 47403
www.westbowpress.com
1 (866) 928-1240

Because of the dynamic nature of the Internet, any web addresses or
links contained in this book may have changed since publication and
may no longer be valid. The views expressed in this work are solely those
of the author and do not necessarily reflect the views of the publisher,
and the publisher hereby disclaims any responsibility for them.

Any people depicted in stock imagery provided by Thinkstock are models,
and such images are being used for illustrative purposes only.
Certain stock imagery © Thinkstock.

ISBN: 978-1-4908-7866-9 (sc)
ISBN: 978-1-4908-7867-6 (e)

Library of Congress Control Number: 2015906991

Print information available on the last page.

WestBow Press rev. date: 05/18/2015

# Contents

# Preface

Finding herself in a place of complete brokenness, Kristy found her way to healing and restoration in a new relationship with God. Previously not having a strong faith, she reached a place of despair, which the Lord used to bring her into a personal relationship with Jesus Christ. He took her life and turned it upside down into a spiral of events that led to a brand new life and mission with Christ. God chases the lost and wounded, and accepts everyone just as they are. She has found God meets everyone right where they are at because His love far outweighs our brokenness. Kristy now teaches about God's revolutionary power and love that allows God to become real to us as individuals, bringing people to a personal level of intimacy with our Creator.

# Introduction

God desires a personal relationship with every one of us, through His Son. We can either accept or deny the ultimate sacrifice that has been provided for us. Many people feel God is far from them or that He has forgotten about them. God has provided the Way for us to know Him intimately and receive His love, but we must acknowledge His free Gift: the gift of Jesus Christ.

Maybe you desire to be closer to God and to really know Him, but you're not sure how. Or, you do know the Lord, but want to go deeper. This book can help you feel closer to our Creator and bring wholeness to your soul if you truly desire this with all your heart and mind.

Jesus was sent to redeem us and to bring us new life. We are required to love Him, accept His sacrifice, and confess that He is Lord. When we learn to seek God diligently and make Him number one, we can find a newness and wholeness we never imagined possible!

We are all chosen by God because of His love. No one is exempt of a richer life when Jesus steps on the scene. When you say "yes" to Christ, your life will be transformed!

*"Therefore if any man be in Christ, he is a new creature: old things are passed away; behold, all things are become new."* 2 Corinthians 5:17 KJV

# Acknowledgement

Thank you to all of you who contributed to make the publication of this book possible. You are a blessing.

# Part I

*Everlasting Life-*
*Increasing intimacy in the Lord,*
*Jesus Christ*

# Chapter 1

# Life

This life we have been given, it is not our own. It comes in all shapes and sizes, yet all our lives are for one divine purpose. We are each called to fulfill a destiny, one that sometimes doesn't even make sense when we begin at the starting line with Jesus. There are leaders, and there are followers. Each member of this body has one main purpose, and that is to fulfill a life with God. Our eyes can only see what He allows us to see at any given time and for a given purpose. From day to day, we are led by something so much greater than anything our minds can fathom. We are led by the almighty hand of God. Our God is one who uplifts us at all times of need, and when we believe that we don't need to listen, this is where God begins with us. This is where the challenge lies, yet at this place, peace surpasses all understanding. This is a place called our true Home which is living a life with Jesus.

When we refuse to give in to the succinct, divine will of the Father, we choose to live a life of denial. This denial manifests into confusion. Without even noticing, we are being blinded by the darkness of the enemy who roams about like a prowling lion, to seek, kill, and destroy us as God's children. The enemy, Satan, has a purpose to kill and destroy until there is no true place left

3

for anything that can house our only Father, our God, who reigns in heaven. Our idle purposes can seem to be the righteous path until we find ourselves in a nation of darkness and a place of being baffled to an extreme. We find ourselves in a place of insignificant clarity; we believe we have found the way, but we are truly lost until we surrender ourselves to the light and let the God given truth from the Heavens be revealed.

Time will reveal all by His mighty right hand that we are glorified and radiant in beauty by our Father. We clearly cannot see the manifestation of His presence until we decide to let go, give in, and let God. Simply said, this is the only way of life, yet we get so confused by the mazes the devil tries to throw at us. His darts become a trigger to our souls, to the brain we have majestically been given; for we are fearfully and wonderfully made (Ps 139:14) by a God who reigns in Heaven. His reign is so large in scope we fail to see the greatness of His glory. A breath of His mouth can move a mountain. Therefore, we can, in turn, move a mountain if we were only to believe the power of the authority we have been unmistakably given (see Mt 17: 20). This power given to all born again Christians, we sadly fail to use. We simply forget that it lies directly within us. Within us we possess the power to change the depths of the sea, to trample amongst all serpents, where we never again have to live a life of worry and defeat. For it is His promise to His children that we shall never be forsaken. His glory and magnitude are so greatly and freely given as a gift of grace that we easily and temporarily look over this God given right, a right freely bestowed to us out of love. Yet, if we harbor bitterness, anger, and resentment, all these ungodly things shall in some form be a hindrance to the blessings.

Take a moment and think about an angry Jesus. The two words, "angry" and "Jesus," are oxymorons. They do not fit together. Comparably, Jesus was one of us: Jesus was a human being made of flesh. However, He was a sinless version of us. He walked this earth as the Son of God with a divine purpose. As He became known to all people His name rang high and true. He was never called to be a person of lesser integrity. His wisdom was unfathomably great because He always kept His eyes directly on the Father. His purpose in life was to fulfill God's destiny, the destiny to save our souls so that we could be free from the pain and anguish we so rightfully deserve. As sinners, we truly deserve a life of eternal punishment. But, because we were given a Savior, a King, we can live and reign here on earth, as Jesus did, and follow in His footsteps to bring an everlasting light and life to those who are still living in the shadows of the darkness. By heaven's light we are called to be a people of humility. We are called to be mild and meek. We are to possess an attitude of respect for the Father, Son, and Holy Ghost. When we come to the realization that we can walk in this same power given to us by Jesus, there is a merciful light at the end of the tunnel. There is a glorious life to be lived by every Christian, where darkness reigns no more; where darkness is pushed back, and light moves forward.

If we are to have a life like Jesus, we must walk and talk like Jesus. Remember WWJD (What Would Jesus Do)? It is a cliché phrase that should always be remembered and an old saying that should never fade. It's a saying we should live by until eternity. When we follow the example of the divinely created Son who lives and reigns for one true purpose, we can ultimately live a life of peace, joy, and happiness.

# Chapter 2

# True Love

In a triumphant world we would all have peace, joy, and understanding without chaos. Silver bells would ring with clarity above our heads and everything would fall into place like puzzle pieces fitting together perfectly. We would know exactly where we are going, what we are called to do, and foresee the future as God has planned it. Consequently, this is just not the way real life is. However, we do have an all-seeing God above us who forever wants to help, guide, and lead us to that perfect light; a perfect God who wants to lead the way into perfection. Perfection is our ultimate destination, a destination into eternity; it is the final resting place called Home.

Being with Jesus can only be a small glimpse in our minds of what this honor must be. His warm, loving heart and kind soul offers total forgiveness no matter where you are at in this earthly life, and must cover for us a great magnitude of feelings. A true honor (of greatest redemption) has been offered by the One who was sinless. He took our place as a sacrifice on the cross. His love for us cannot even be described in words! A true, everlasting friend who sincerely and truly laid down His life for His friends cannot be found in this life. This profound love is only offered by Jesus Christ. It seems something too good to be real, a figment of our imaginations. This great, unthinkable offer was made holy and is a true sacrifice by our Father in Heaven, who never leaves us nor forsakes us. He is the One who does not see us by our faults, but only as pure, holy images of His begotten Son. Through the Son we must come to know and love to live the life that is so freely offered by the grace and mercy of God.

God's grace in our lives is an unthinkable act in a world of fleshly hearts and desires; a free gift offered for us, who have sinned against Him. Our humanness subjects us to continue to quarrel for our own selfish desires. Free gifts with no strings attached are hard to come by. When we learn to openly receive this free grace of God, locking our hands into His hand which is always extended down to us, our lives supernaturally begin to change and we are touched by the One who loved us first, Jesus Christ.

When we can let go, and let God, our lives completely change to a wholeness never before known or felt to mankind. Prior, we only know and feel what we have been taught, or have lacked. Living this life to be perfect and pleasing to others instead of God will only dig us deeper into the pit of destruction. Once we have learned to reverently fear and love our gracious Father in heaven, He will teach us His proper way of being a blessing to others in love. Only then will our graciousness be evident to all, simply because we have freely received His grace.

This true and proper worship of our God is much more rewarding and pleasing than our striving to be perfect in order to appeal to Him. He accepts and loves us just as we are! He knows our mistakes and failures before we make them. Yet, He chooses to love us still, compassionately, with His whole heart, no ifs ands or buts. There is nothing we can do to make Him love us more; all we need to do is to come to Him, receiving His open arms, and receive the grace He is offering. As we choose to let Him guide us through our journey in this life, we begin to have clarity and a targeted purpose. When one finds the true God given purpose of his or her life, life will have a new meaning. This life will be filled with zeal and the passion to serve with a new heart, a heart that no longer thinks of itself, but seeks to find a deeper meaning of life. This heart will honor, first and foremost, God and His trinity, followed by a true love and the service of God's people on Earth.

We are all created in the likeness of His image and therefore have been implanted with the spiritual desire to love and serve Him with our whole heart. It is up to us to make the decision as to whether or not we will receive Him and be obedient to His calling, or to suppress His voice and the love He is desperately trying to make us hear. Again, I reiterate, it is up to us to make the choice to take His hand and follow in His footsteps, or to continue in our own selfish lives to a place of no purpose or true fulfillment. Once we decide, our path will start to unwind.

# Chapter 3

# Freely Receive

If it were to be that by our own grace we could be saved and live a life of glory, then we would not need a heavenly Savior who always understands our needs. It is then not by our own grace that we are saved, but by the blood of Jesus and by God's saving grace; we are free to come to Him and enter His rest. His definition of rest looks much differently than ours.

If we say that we have no sin, then we have deceived ourselves. But when we come to God boldly believing in His magnificent promise of everlasting eternal life, we are free to come to Him without mockery, judgment or criticism. We can then enter a place of peace and heartfelt compassion of our Savior. After all, isn't it purely love we are all seeking? We inherently crave a warm love to satisfy the heart, and only God's warm love can melt the icy, stone cold hearts of us as sinners.

When we accept His free compliment of grace, we also are entitled to receive His free mercy, bestowed upon us by His own free will. A purchase has been made for us and to us by the right of Jesus' blood to sanctify and make us holy for one succinct purpose, and that is to fulfill the life of God. As we come into His open arms, we receive the healing and rest simply offered with the loving heart of our Heavenly Father. We do not need to be in fear that He will reject us or ignore our wishes. His promise to give us the secret desires of our hearts intercedes from Jesus, even when we don't know how to ask or what we truly need to break free and heal the bondages. We ourselves have created bondage through acts of being disobedient to God. Yet, thankfully, when we come to Him and simply receive His Son, He will wash it all away and never remind us of these transgressions again! What more could a hurting soul ask for from their parent and guardian?

*"The Lord your God is in the midst of you, a Mighty One, a Savior [Who saves]! He will rejoice over you with joy; He will rest [in silent satisfaction] and in His love He will be silent and make no mention [of past sins, or even recall them]; He will exult over you with singing."*
(Zephaniah 3:17 AMP)

Not too much can compare to the glory that is given to us as a co-heir of Jesus Christ, the High Priest. He understands us and was tempted in all the same ways we are tempted, from birth until we pass on to the eternal, everlasting life of freedom with our glorious Father. We shall boldly and aggressively approach Him in His true nature because He will never reject us or turn us away. All we are called to do is believe and try our best while He does the rest for us! That is plainly why we Christians are called "Believers". We are saints who want to please a Father we cannot see, but who we entrust our lives to, because He loved us first. He loved us enough to send His only Son to die for us while we were still sinners, living a life in ignorance to Christ. This is a plain, yet underestimated statement of a proper love of God that cannot be fathomed or understood in our own consciences. Our job then is not to understand, but go to Him, receive His Son, receive His great favor and abundance, and love Him with all our hearts. When we do, we are in for a joy ride in life that can never be expected! Our lives will be filled with unexplainable joy and passion that cannot be from anyone other than from the right hand of our God in heaven.

# Chapter 4

# Seasons

As seasons change, so can our relationship with Jesus. The way we live our lives can either please or displease God, yet it never leaves Him mad at us. He only chastises to guide, lead, and direct us to the best life He already has planned out for us. Whether or not we listen is one of the pieces left for us to decide.

As a tree turns brown and starts to wither in the fall, so can the season of a part of our lives if we are not careful to consistently seek and follow the guiding and promptings of God's Holy Spirit. The Holy Ghost has been freely provided to us as a helping hand to understand God's will for our lives. If we become aware that His Holy Spirit is always there once we accept Jesus as our Savior and freely become born again by the grace of God, we then start a journey in life that is indescribable in joy and happiness! Now that is not to say that all things God takes us through will be joyful and happy, but everything we go through in each season of life is for some specific, divine purpose. It will lead us to a better and greater place within ourselves. We are each being led specifically down every road or path we travel by God. As we abide in Him, He will lead us to and through the next specific season of life. Some paths may be less exciting, or less fun and painful, while some may even take us to a place of confronting fear. Our job then is to stand firm in faith and keep on believing God will get us through it. We can rest in knowing that all things can in some way, create a stronger character within us, build a deeper relationship with God our Father, and strengthen the faith muscles we never knew we have.

Each season is a new journey. Each will come to an end, and a new one will begin. That's the cycle of life until Jesus comes to take us home. It is your decision to enjoy this ride of life and each particular season, no matter what the circumstance. It's up to you to keep the faith that God has everything under control. Or, you can choose to be miserable and barely make it through each day with a chip on your shoulder, being angry at life and people as it quickly passes you by.

Sometimes we just need to get to a place of complacency where we completely entrust our lives and our whole being in the hands of the One who knows all. We may be called to simply enjoy the gift of life that has been bought and paid for by a price (the blood of Jesus), and to enjoy each day the Lord has provided because we are His creation. You are a creature fearfully and wonderfully made, a true and righteous creature dearly loved by God. You were created for a specific purpose, a specific destiny, and to be a personal representation of God our Father, in Jesus Christ, the holy Son of God.

We have a purpose here, and it is not for ourselves. When we become less self-focused and realize we are here on this earth right now, in this time, to serve a purpose and a mission for the Creator of the universe, our life begins! We are new, old things have passed away (2 Co 5:17), and we can begin to live a life of excellence. We begin a new purpose driven life and can confidently say, "Here I am Lord. Show me my path. Teach me your will for the life you have given me." It is then that we release His boundless glory to be put into action and to go to work. We can march ahead to start being the light and begin shining bright upon others until they can see the beams of brightness radiating from inside us. The inner beauty of Jesus now starts to shine forth, and the journey of a miraculous life can begin!

# Chapter 5

# The Light

Our destiny holds a new realm when our human creativity becomes meshed with the divine Spirit of God's creativeness. Once the freeness of God's Spirit is unleashed within our personal spirit, the hourglass of life is turned upwards to deliver a new lease on life. Our passion for living, combined with a complete sense of humbleness and freedom, allows us to create and aspire to be a legacy of the realm of Jesus Christ; our lives are now taken to a new level.

An intense desire and burning passion laced with zeal for life can create the freedom to be like no one else and to go where not one single soul has gone before. Once we reach the freedom to be specifically who God has created us to be, no one on planet Earth can stop this person you are called to be.

The healing that penetrates from a wounded soul becomes unleashed. Divine pretenses can properly function, astounding others with this great, new way of life. Each organism created straight from the heavenly realm of a right hand greater than we can ever fathom, is a new creature of life, one in which all the old has passed away and all becomes new. In reality, the temptation to try things in our own strength is strong, but apart from God we can do nothing. We must listen in obedience. Apart from Jesus, the inner man cannot function, and finds no distinct purpose for this lifetime. Although when the two meet, heaven releases a brand new song! A song of new light and life by the Author and Finisher of the universe is born.

Let's visualize a house. Each house on a hill radiates with light as long as one does not turn the light off. Each pre-ordained, destined, God given journey radiates a light and those who do know Jesus can easily see this is a different light. This is a light many others do not have. But if the light is turned off and suppressed, the freedom of creativity will not flow, and the Creator of the universe cannot work through us.

You are as close to God, or anything for that matter, as you want to be. If your life lacks a feeling of completeness, God is missing in some way. Jesus cannot live where there is no light. Darkness always gives way to the light. When you want the light, you shall find it. Jesus never turns down a hungry soul. Our Creator can work and be revealed in glory where there is light. Never turn the light out.

# Chapter 6

# Born Again

In Jesus' name we have the right to freely and boldly approach the throne of God. His character is meek and mild, and we must seek Him diligently with all our heart, all our soul, and our entire mind. When we truly radically love Him, we are transformed to a new creation in whole, and nothing, not even the powerful enemy, can stop or postpone this change.

When we walk in love there is a fresh, new power given to us that cannot be walked out in the flesh. This type of love can only come from the Righteous One who is love: our God. When we are filled with His Spirit we receive His agape love. This type of love is never ceasing, never ending, and never loses a fight. We become the righteousness of Jesus Christ Himself, because we are blood bought children, purchased by the death of Jesus. What then has washed away our sin completely? Only the blood of Jesus has done so. We must give honor and respect to Jesus, and to the blood on the cross He shed the day of His death. But, His death meant life. His death was a resurrection to a new life paid for by the One true Father who knows our hearts and deeply loves us as His own children.

To be a child of the most High God is truly a privilege. It is the highest honor one could ever wish for, but unless you know how to use that honor and walk in it, you will still be left powerless in the dark.

Pushing back the enemy is a true challenge. It is real and must be fought in battle by putting on the full armor of God. Ephesians 6:11 states, *"Put on the full armor of God, so that you can take your stand against the devil's schemes."* We must fight not against people, but the enemy's evil ways working throughout the earth (for study see Eph 6:10-18). The devil is real, and until you fully accept that he is a real power who does roam this earth, you will be left powerless to fight back. We can rest assured that we will always win the battle against Satan, not because of our own strength, but because in Jesus Christ we have been given authority over all the wicked powers that roam and lurk about trying to devour us.

By putting on the full armor of God we no longer have to walk in fear because God's perfect love for us casts out all fear (1 Jn 4:18). His perfect love for us is pure righteousness that can never lose a fight. When we walk in step with Him, He fights our battles for us, and He never gives up on us. The problem appears when we decide to give up on Him. Have you given up on God? Or do you still keep your faith? Is there a situation you are facing in your life right now that looks and seems impossible? I challenge you to start seeking God about it once again. Maybe you feel like God wasn't hearing you, or He was ignoring you because you thought you weren't important enough. I can promise you, this is not God. God always hears, and always listens intently. *All* things are possible with God (Mt 19:26). God does not have time limits. We make the time limits on God's work. His answer is sometimes simply, "Not yet." Our job is to seek Him whole heartedly for His will for us, to love Him with our whole heart, and to believe, which means to keep our faith in Him at all times. Is there a promise you have given up on because it seems to you it's taking too long? Or perhaps the devil has convinced you that something is too good to be true for you. Maybe you're hearing that you're not worth it and not valuable enough to God for Him to take time for you in your life.

The devil is a liar, and I challenge you to seek God whole heartedly once again in your situation, and listen. Listen to His will because He wants what is best for you. He can see things you can't and He always has your best interest at the center of His heart. Nothing you have done is so bad that God will not love you. He wants to love you. We are the ones that make it tough for Him to love us at times. Do not give up on God or the wonderful life He has planned for you. Jesus Christ Himself has died on the cross and shed His own blood for you to have the beautiful, abundant life He has always had planned for you. The truth and beauty God tries to give us is exactly what the devil eagerly tries to steal. You deserve Jesus' beautiful plan because you are a child of God.

If you have not yet received Jesus Christ as your personal Savior, He is anxiously awaiting for you to come to Him! Just ask. Stop right now and ask Jesus to come into your life. Ask Him to forgive you of all your sins and wash you clean with His blood. Ask Him to make you His newborn child. That's all it takes, a simple heartfelt surrender to the One who has always loved you first!

# Chapter 7

# Believe

J esus promised that when He left this place called earth, and ascended to be with the Father in heaven, we would be able to do even greater things than He Himself had done (Jn 14:12). As a follower and seeker of Jesus Christ, what a strong, powerful promise we have! Do you believe it?

This is where some people hinder their own power in Jesus, with a simple lack of belief. Belief is faith. Faith is belief. Faith believes in what you cannot see. It doesn't take much faith to believe what you can already physically see in the natural (with your eyes). We must call out into existence the promises of God to us as His children. Speak it out loud. It is not enough to sit idly by and wish and hope for things to happen by the will of God. He cannot, and will not work without faith and a strong belief that He will fulfill His promises.

Maybe you don't know about the promises of God. Maybe you feel like God's promises are too good for you. Think again. If you have accepted Jesus as your Savior, every single promise in the Bible is for you! It is filled with unbelievably exciting scripture for you to read and speak forth into your own life, but you must believe it. You must also study and read the Bible. Sometimes this can feel like an overwhelming task, but it is not meant to be. It is an exciting journey to learn all that we can have as believers and true followers of Jesus Christ.

Maybe you're thinking, "I don't know how to read and study the Bible, let alone even where to begin." Let me reassure you, you are not alone, and God will help you. He knows you have made a decision to want to learn about Him and read His word, so simply ask that He will help you. There is no better time to start than right now. Don't put God aside one more day, but let's make it clear, we are not to learn and seek Him only for what we can get from Him. We need to read, study, and seek Him because we love Him, need Him, and want to know Him like a family member or a close friend. We need to see Him as someone we can love and trust; someone who knows our deepest desires and knows everything about us. Why? Because He loves us! He created you by His own hand in your mother's womb (Ps 139: 13), and He does not make mistakes. He knew you before you were born (Jer 1:5). He knew everything about you and your life before you did, before you even came to life (see Eph 1:11). God is love. All He wants is for you to love Him in return and to believe in Him because He never leaves us.

As we learn through His word in the Bible who He is and all the amazing things He wants to give us, we can become bolder in the way we believe. We start to believe His promises are exactly for us and we can start asking Him for His greatness. Live large, not small! Believe that He is, and that He rewards those who diligently seek Him. Begin to learn who He is and seek to be closer to Him so you know Him with intimacy. Don't just seek the blessings He can give you. If your number one desire is to love Him and get close to Him while abiding in His will for your life, He will freely give you blessings as His great reward.

# Chapter 8

# Transform

As we transform to the likeness of the Son, Jesus Christ, our wills and ways no longer become about us. Until we receive Jesus and invite Him into our lives, there is no true meaning or purpose, and it seems we wander around aimlessly looking for a purpose in life, something that will fulfill us. Let's fast forward to after accepting and surrendering to Jesus - light bulb moment! Clarity arises, peace begins, and we find rest just from believing in our true Savior, in knowing that He reigns forevermore.

To believe in something or someone who is unseen seems far out in the realm of reality to unbelievers. Yet as followers and believers of Jesus Christ, there is no option other than to believe He exists. We know that He is, and always will be. When we take our eyes off God, this is when things become confusing. Our lives quickly begin to fall apart. Until we realize we are nothing without Him, we will never fully do the things in life we want to do. The puzzle pieces cannot fit together unless Christ is the center of all that we partake.

God will provide the way. This is the provision of our Master. We need not know how, but we need to know that He will, if it is His will for us. He is a good and just God. He will give us what's right for us and hold what is not because He loves us. God, and only God, is all seeing. He knows exactly where, when and how. He places a protective shield around us as born again believers so we do not have to worry. Jesus came so we might have life in abundance and enjoy it.

Many times we let the enemy steal the joy Jesus wants to give us. It all comes down to a choice we must make. Are you going to follow Jesus or follow the devil's bait? It's an easy choice, but walking it out is the challenge at times. That's one of the many reasons we need Jesus. He helps us at all times and never leaves our side because God's promise is to never leave or forsake us. *Never!* What a bold promise we can always rely on! God does not break His promises. His character is integrity and love. He cannot be mocked (Gal 6:7). He is a rewarder to those who diligently seek Him (Heb 11:6). This means you must make the effort to chase Him in all things and at all times. Possibly, you find yourself asking, "How do I do that?" He will help you. Ask Him. We cannot follow Him on our own. We need His help to walk in His ways and do His will.

This is called surrendering. Surrender yourself to the One who has called you into existence. Surrender your being to the One who loved you first. Maybe that word or instruction makes you feel uneasy or uncomfortable. Maybe you don't know what it means. All of these feelings are normal. Simply ask and invite God in His fullness into your life. The leading of His Holy Spirit fills your inner being and lives in you; you will be led by the most powerful leadership in the entire universe! That righteous power resides in you at all times. You can access it at any time, and you can live by this if you allow it. This means packing up your own feelings, putting them in a suitcase and shipping them off. This is dying to self. It's dying to your own natural, worldly, fleshy feelings and desires. It is being dependent upon someone who knows you better and loves you more than you could possibly dream or imagine. With God, and His leadership of the Holy Spirit, nothing is impossible (Mt 19:26). You may see, do, or feel things you never thought possible.

There is one requirement: you must believe and be unwavering in your faith. God does not provide abundantly to those who are filled with doubt and unbelief in Him. When you get tired and exhausted of the life you have and realize your ways are not working, that is also the time to realize God has been waiting ever so patiently for you to come to Him instead of selfishly living your own life; invite Him in so that He may begin to work. God cannot and will not work when you are trying to run your own life. It does not work like that in His realm because He is the One in control. When you invite Him in and unleash Him to lead you and guide you, the Holy Spirit's power can also be unleashed unto you and your life, but you must allow it. We can't hold Him back from His work. Remember, God always knows what's best. *We do not.*

Being led by the Holy Spirit and following Him in our lives is the missing piece for many Christians. They may have God and Jesus, but are not following the leadership of The Holy Spirit, and receiving the great excitement that happens as a result of the Holy Spirit.

# Chapter 9

# Come To Me

Scripture tells us to submit to God first, resist the devil and he will flee (see Jas 4:7). My question for you is, have you submitted to God? The word *submit* means to yield to governance or authority. Yield, by one definition, means to surrender or relinquish to the physical control of another: to surrender or submit (oneself) to another (Merriam-Webster dictionary). We must remember we are not in control of ourselves. There is only one being that is to have control over us and that is God.

What does it mean to give up control of running our own lives and surrendering it to the One who loves us more than we can possibly imagine? In simple words, I believe it means to let go. Now that doesn't mean to live a life of carelessness, but rather, to give our cares to God. To pray, seek, ask, look to, and yield to our heavenly Father at ALL times and in ALL things. Keep in mind consistently that He is the One who knows what's best for us and the One who knows all. He is the Author and Finisher, the Beginning and End. Wouldn't it make much more sense to put Him in the control center seat of our life like a pilot having all the controls of the airplane? Nothing happens, and you will not reach your destination without that pilot.

What God wants is for you to trust Him, not just in some things, but *all* things. We can't pick and choose which areas we want to relinquish control to Him. He wants total control; not to be controlling, but because He loves us and He wants us to be happy with our life. He sees the big picture, not just here and now. He is constantly trying to guide us into the best in all areas of our life. We are His children and His family.

Why does this tend to be so hard for us? We are used to taking care of ourselves in life. We are used to running our own lives and trying to figure out our own problems. But guess what? That is not the way God wants us to run our lives. That does not show we are trusting in Him. That shows we are trusting in ourselves only, and our own strength. Jesus said apart from Him we can do nothing (Jn 15:5). God also states that we shall not lack any beneficial thing (Ps 34:10). Yet, we still think we can do things through our own strength. We cannot make things happen without Him, not in any way.

Submission is not an easy thing for us as humans. We all want to be in charge and think we are okay. Sometimes it takes until we are so miserable or hit a wall of tragedy in our lives, for us to realize we are not the ones in charge, and we can finally submit and ask God to take control. We allow Him to take over, to help, guide, and fix all the broken pieces we have created. Because He loves us, He is always right there waiting to take our hand and pull us up out of the pit we have created, along with giving us His gift of healing our wounds. We create our own pits, not God, or anyone else. Part of this healing is taking responsibility for our actions, and we can take comfort in knowing He loves to help us break free. Jesus invites us with His words, *"Come to Me, all you who labor and are heavy-laden and overburdened, and I will cause you to rest. [I will ease and relieve and refresh your souls.]"* (Mt 11:28 AMP) He heals up our wounds and binds us back together into complete wholeness, something we can never experience without Jesus.

"Rest" is a great word of comfort. I believe it is when we try to run our own lives, doing what we want to do, that we create busyness with no true purpose, chaos, destruction, anxiety, worry, depression, addictions, hate, and the list goes on. We are not listening and submitting to God and His plan for us. That's when our lives become chaotic, miserable, and crazy. I will stress the point, do not blame God. We must listen and submit. We must do both. You may hear or feel deep inside what He wants you to do to straighten out your life, whether something big or small, but are you really listening and doing what He is prompting you to do?

He will never force us to do anything; He has given us a free will. He wants us to choose Him over everything else, but He lets us make our own decisions. He wants us to choose to listen to Him while giving Him control. He desires for us to love and trust Him enough to submit to His ways. He wants this so much for each of His children, and we are all His children, every single one of us, including you! He helps us to desire Him and follow His ways through the gift of His Holy Spirit. That is love!

# Chapter 10

# God is Love

We have one true Master and one true purpose in life. That is God and God alone. That may seem overbearing, but it certainly is not His intention. God is the answer. God is what we are constantly searching for everywhere else in our lives, whether it's in other people or things.

Jesus came so you may have life in abundance, life to the fullest (Jn 10:10). This is a promise if we chose to take Him up on His offer. His character and integrity are unfailing in love. In Christ alone we can walk by faith and discover who we truly are and are meant to be. Nothing but this light matters when we enter into the rest of God. With a clean, fresh slate of a new, infused life of light, we can conquer whatever task is laid before us. The same power and Spirit that raised Jesus from the dead lives inside us as Believers! (For study see Eph 1:19-22) To say that we are anything less than conquerors, is an understatement. *"I can do all things through Christ who strengthens me"* (Php 4: 13) becomes the motto for this new life we have freely received.

Although we have freely received, we are now required to freely give. We are to freely and openly give the love to others that Jesus gave to us and offer His mercy and loving kindness without question, without a thought. His pure love should be the motive to live a life of serving others. The conquest of our worldly life is not to please ourselves, but to love God and to love others. Isn't that what we all want deep down, to be loved?

Love is not just a feeling. It is an action. Love is a thought, word, or deed in giving the extra effort to show you care. Jesus was, and is our prime example of love throughout the Bible, and He is alive and well today. Loving can be walked out in many areas of our lives, but true and proper worship is to act like Jesus. What would Jesus do? If you know His beautiful character, you know that His one true inner motive is always to love.

With Him you will never find hurt. With Him you will never be forsaken. In Him there is always comfort. The list is never ending in His ways of goodness. If you are hurting, Jesus is the way. Seek Him and follow Him, and He will know how to provide rest. As vast as the shores of the sea, Jesus' love cannot be compared. It is endless and never stops flowing into your heart. The healing from the hurts we have suffered can only come from the understanding of the wounds He suffered physically, emotionally, and mentally. Jesus suffered. Jesus suffered more than any one of us on this earth. Yet we somehow seem to think our lives at times are the worst, and no one could possibly understand. There is One who always understands: Jesus.

God sent His only Son to die on the cross for each and every one of us (see Jn 3:16). He sent His own flesh and blood to suffer and die for us so that we might be reconciled to Him. God's love is pure and never ending. Imagine sending your loved one to be beaten and hung on a cross to die in order to save someone else who didn't deserve it. God's love is true, and His heart is golden. As a father, I'm sure His heart hurt so badly to watch His Son go through this pain because we are all sinners in need of a Savior. Yet He still chose to send His Son. Jesus loves us so much that He chose to die for us, even though we were sinners. Although some still do not believe in Him, reject, or mock Him, He still loves every single one of His people all the same.

God said, *"Everything under heaven belongs to Me"* (Job 41: 11). He chooses to love all. Our lives can never be straightened out or make sense if we continue to remove God from the world. This is clearly not the answer. We need more of Him and more of His love working through us everywhere we turn.

# Chapter 11

# Intimacy

When Jesus invited us to take up our cross and follow Him (see Mk 8:34-38), in essence, He revealed that doing what He asked will promptly bring about change. You will not remain the same. One thing to keep in the forefront of your mind as reality is that God cannot help you if you will not help yourself. If you are not willing to listen and change despite being aware of His light, He will not be able to help. We are the clay, He is the potter. He cannot mold something hard and unwilling into a piece of art. He needs moldable people that truly want His help and are willing to sacrifice selfish desires to let go and give Him control.

Be *transformed* by the renewing of your mind (Ro 12:2). We will absolutely need to submit to our wonderful Father who disciplines us because He loves us too much to leave us alone. He cares too much to sit back and watch us struggle forever, but remember, He will never force anyone against their own free will. He will never leave us hang, but He will not impose on us and go to work until we put Him in the driver's seat of our lives.

Will this be easy? Not always. Could it be painful? Sometimes, but He always knows what is best for every individual He's ever created. Just when we think we know and understand, we probably don't. Everything happens for a reason. It is not our responsibility to always know why or how, but to trust in faith in the One who knows us inside and out. God does not make mistakes, which brings up the clear fact that you are not a mistake either. God creates beauty, not garbage. God creates perfection, not junk. We are made and seen as perfection by Jesus Christ. God works with us until the day Jesus comes to take us to heaven, by bringing us to that place of perfection in Jesus. We need Jesus all the time to help us be perfected. We can lean on Him and rely on Him at all times, for all things.

By Jesus' blood we are washed clean (Heb 10:22). Our sins are forgiven. By grace, we have been saved through faith (Eph 2:8). Without the blood of Jesus, there is no chance we would last one day, one minute or one second. Before we begin our journey with Christ, we think that we can tackle life's problems and dilemmas; but, only in time do we come to realize He was the One holding us up all along. We never really take care of ourselves on our own, and all the times we may try, we can't do a good job at it because we are nothing without Him. When we accept Jesus as our Savior and let Him in our lives, we understand we are fearfully and wonderfully made (Ps 139:14). We are perfection in God's eyes through Jesus Christ. We just need some tweaking.

Of course this takes time. God is very good in His character. He gives us all the time in the world. He'll never leave us or give up on us, no matter if and when we mess up. He is so good to each and every one of us all the time. He is all around us, covering us with His love. Look around you. His majestic beauty is everywhere. It brings a clear sense of awe. He adorns this world with a beautiful touch of love everywhere we look. To really know Him is the greatest beauty of all!

Do you know Him? Or do you just know of Him and know His name? One thing He is *not* is a magic genie waiting for someone to rub His lamp so He can grant wishes. He is a God of intimate relationship and fellowship. He does not want just an hour of your time on Sunday and to be asked for some favors, just to be pushed aside until next Sunday's church service. He desires to deeply know each and every single one of us, not for what He can do for us, but for a relationship where we desire to know Him and who He is. He desires for us to know His character and to be His best friend, His partner, His son or daughter, and to love Him in reverent fear. That does not mean we should ever be afraid of Him. He is not a scary being to shy away from, but to fear Him in awe of His great power, glory, and might; to know that His power is unspeakable, yet always just, and full of compassion. He longs to intimately know each of us, but we make the choice to take His offer and get to know Him while building a relationship with Him, or to ignore His hand offered to us. If we so foolishly choose, we can go our own way. He desires to lavish His love upon us (see 1 Jn 3:1) and we simply can reach out to say yes with an open heart, but we must be ready to listen.

## Chapter 12

# A Choice

When you look inside your heart, what do you feel? Is it a long lasting friendship with yourself, or is it hatred, anger, or a feeling that you are of little value? Each piece of a broken heart is like a torn, ripped piece of clothing that needs mending. When we submerse ourselves in Jesus' love, we can begin to repair the broken pieces and wounds that lay beneath the surface. If you feel you have never suffered a "misplaced" heart, take some quiet time to spend with yourself. Sometimes troubled hearts are broken, but we are deceived into thinking everything is fine, when on the inside everything is actually falling apart, waiting for eternal restoration that can only come from a love above.

What does this love look and feel like? The fun part is that it's different for everyone. Jesus' relationship with every individual is unique. That is why we cannot get stuck in the trap of comparing ourselves to others. None of us are alike. We are individually crafted just the way God wants us to be, which is why He made us and chose us to be the way we are. Once we understand that we can begin to love ourselves in a holy way, the way God wants us to; not with boastful, arrogant pride, but with a meek and mild love of self that represents the heart and soul of Jesus Christ.

God does not want us to hate or demoralize ourselves; yet many of us choose a self-destructive path that breaks God's heart. We must choose the path of righteousness and remember that we belong to God. We are to highly value ourselves because He does, and because He gave us life. He breathed life into us and we became man. He died through His only Son, so that we may have eternal life. We are not called to do anything less than to love ourselves.

So what does it look like to love oneself? Love of self means we are not critical or judgmental and have no inner loathing; we are peaceful, content, and full of joy. We are prosperous because we live a life with Jesus and acknowledge it. We desire to please God so His love and warmth fills our hearts. Life can be viewed as a special gift because we fall deeply in love with Jesus. He fills the empty space in our inner being with His gleaming power of happiness. We become empowered with the enlightenment to go through trials and tribulations because when we are weak, God is strong (2 Co 12:9). We get a chance to watch God work firsthand. We get to see His glory revealed within us and around us, simply because He is a loving God and He wants us to know His love for us.

Sometimes there is a miraculous provision or answer. Other times, it's deliverance by taking us right through the fire, although we never get burned. He teaches, disciplines, and chastises so we learn, respect, revere, honor, and love Him. He builds character and a higher being within us, all to glorify Him through us. He is a sovereign, just God, and His love is so deep it cannot be put into words. It flows outwardly like a stream that gushes forth to become a waterfall of passion.

35

When we live a life to please God, we are surrounded with so called miracles every day. It's a matter of opening our eyes to see them and not pass things off as coincidence. God blesses us many times over, yet we do not always give Him due credit. When we look to see His glory all around us, the world becomes a much sweeter place. Life becomes much more pleasurable, and His hand of peace is upon us.

We reap what we sow (see Gal 6:7). What are you planting in your life? Are you harboring feelings of bitterness, sourness, hostility, chaos, or peace, tranquility, happiness, and joy? Life is not made by the circumstances in our life. Our life is created by us. It's what we make of it and how we choose to react at whatever comes our way. Life is an attitude that brings us an inner peace, joy, and hope that no one can take away despite seemingly chaotic circumstances. These upbeat feelings come from being a true believer and follower of Jesus Christ. We know that no matter what life's troubles are, God is always holding us up. He is fighting our battles for us. How we react and whether or not we choose to trust and lean on Him will make or break a person in the roller coaster of life. It will determine whether you stand in glory on top of the mountain peak, praising His glorious name, or sink to the bottom continually trying to climb your way through quicksand to the top, over and over again, making no true gain.

This journey of life is a bunch of tests. We will go through them all our lives. Our job is to go through them with a good attitude and pass each test. If we do, we move to a new level and another test because this produces perseverance, character, faith and trust in Him. We need to trust God in faith and keep following Him no matter what; this means "dying to self". We forget about our own feelings and press on to seek God's will. Each test develops our character and gets us closer to the path of purpose He has chosen for us. At the same time, this brings us closer to Him. Again, we can't be, or do anything apart from him, so always ask God to help you be obedient to His will.

# Chapter 13

# Answer the Door

It is by God's grace that we have been saved through faith in Jesus Christ the Messiah. How then, can we believe we have any right to claim God's promises by our own works of flesh or faith? We don't, and we must come to God alone and thank him relentlessly by praising, worshipping, and giving Him thanks continuously for the precious gift of His Son, Jesus Christ, who has paid this holy price for us. Nothing we will ever do will make God love us more. It is then by this freedom that we are called to know and receive His glorious love and walk in it every single day so that we may know our God-given identity as "in Christ". We can claim every promise God has ever spoken by His word and receive it as our own. This causes us to remain thankful to Him and to Jesus, who is the Author and Finisher of our faith. We come to Him boldly because we know we have been adopted into sonship by our Savior's punishment. By Jesus dying on the cross and taking the punishment we deserve, we no longer receive punishment for our sins.

We needed a Savior to be forgiven of God's wrath, and *"God so loved the world that He gave His only begotten Son, so that whoever believes in Him shall not perish but have everlasting life"* (Jn 3:16). We do not get our rightly deserved punishment because Jesus chose

38

to take our place. He chose to take our punishment and hear our cries. He chose to be beaten and hung to death on the cross for you and every soul on this earth. Whether you are a new believer or a believer for many years, He lovingly makes the same offer to anyone who believes in Him. You do not have to do work or do anything in order for Him to love you. He just does! And what He wants is your love in return.

All that must be done is to ask that Jesus come into our lives by His Holy Spirit, in whom we must believe in, even though He cannot physically be seen. I believe it is a glorious day for Jesus when a person decides to ask Him to come into one's own life, receive Him by faith, and ask Him to forgive them of their sins.

We are all guilty of sin, but in God's eyes no one person's sin is worse than that of another. He wants us to believe in Him and love Him with our whole heart. He desires us. He desires to envelop us with His love. He desires to know us intimately. He loved us first, and because of this love, we will want to, in time, do things to please Him. He will help us to do this, so if you don't yet have that feeling of "want to" do not be ashamed. We can do nothing without Him, so start asking Him to help you and your personal desires. He knows our hearts. He knows if your heart is right and He admires that.

This is a journey we are on and the journey will continuously change you because God is continuously working in us, even when we don't know or feel it. We just need to have a willing heart that says, "Yes God, I want and need your help." God hears you and knows you better than anyone ever could. He knows when you rise up and lie down (see Ps 139:1-4). He enjoys you and enjoys knowing you. If you feel like nobody loves or cares about you, God does; you must believe that because you are living on this earth today. God created you. God brought you here for a reason. His biggest reason is because He loves you and needs you. Jesus loves you. Jesus is the friend who died for you. He took your punishment as His own. He laid down His life for you as your friend (Jn 15:12-13). He chose this. No one forced Him to do so. He chose you. You are never alone, and God is always with you. Let Him love you.

It is possible you are already a believer but you are keeping areas of your life cut off from God. Let Him in. Don't hold anything back from your heavenly Father who wants to have relationship, fellowship, and companionship with you more than anything else. He wants you. When you let Him in completely, you will sense Him and feel Him near, greater than ever before. Jesus is knocking on the door of your home, the inner you. Will you turn the door knob and allow Him to come in? Invite Him with your words of acceptance and He will come near to you. He will not force His way into your heart. He waits for you to ask. God will teach you how to love Him with your whole heart.

# Chapter 14

## Blind Eyes Cannot See

Blind eyes can't see. I'm not talking about being physically blind, but spiritually being blind. What is the true cause? Deception by the enemy of this world causes deceit and a blinding of the truth. Satan roams about like a roaring lion, seeking to devour us (1 Pe 5:8). When we come to a place of truth, which is in Jesus Christ alone, our eyes that have been blinded from torment are now opened to see what we could never see before.

The life of the spiritually blind is all around us. Even believers in Christ may still be living in a spiritually blind world. Isn't it our place then as believers in Jesus to seek the life God has called us to have? Isn't it our place to fulfill the purposes God has set before us? Absolutely! But only until we are willing to step aside and die to self along with our own emotional feelings and desires, can we step out and boldly go where we never believed we could go. We are more than conquerors in Christ. In Him, our eyes are opened. In Him, we have the truth about ourselves. In Him, we once were blind, but now we see. Only in Christ alone can we live the life of freedom He desperately wants us to have.

Surrender all. That means to give yourself and all your possessions to the One who knows you best, for His purposes. In Him we can passionately love and receive healing from the wounds we desire to be free from. Any pain and anguish you are suffering or have suffered is not "yours"; it does not belong to you. It is only a part of life that is being used to shape and mold you to be a stronger and better you. Do not claim the hardships as your own. They are only for a season. They too shall pass. Your hardships will be conquered in and with Christ, but you must believe this. God works through faith. He heals the brokenhearted and binds up their wounds (Ps 147:3). But God cannot work unless you believe in Him and believe He has the power to do so. God will not and cannot work in a life filled with consistent doubt.

Have you ever had someone in your life that did not believe in you and it left you feeling low and saddened? Or perhaps you did have the support and belief of others and it gave you feelings of empowerment and strength. This is how God works. He is almighty and omnipotent, everywhere, all the time, but He will only work by the faith that you put in Him. Faith opens doors and releases His hand of favor. Faith pours out His strength upon you. Seeing does not believe; believing is seeing. When you believe in what you cannot see according to God's will and purpose, He is most pleased. He rewards those who *diligently* seek Him, not just in times of need or only on church days, but consistently seek Him for who He is.

God is all-seeing and never fails. Believe in His strength and you will see His works prevail in your life. When our eyes are watching and waiting for the spiritual glory of His all-powerful hand of might and favor, we begin to see a place of natural peace and healing filled with blessings. Until we open our eyes and hearts to Him we will remain blind in an enemy driven world of spiritual torment. We can choose to seek God and follow His ways while believing in His glory, or we can choose to follow the enemy of darkness. In this darkness we will continue being deceived and blinded to the light and truth of Jesus Christ.

God knows and rewards those who choose to follow Him. He knows the desires of our hearts. When you choose to no longer remain blinded and give yourself to the Lord, your spiritual eyes will be opened. He will appear to you in new ways and healing can then begin.

# Chapter 15

# Beauty for Ashes

Do you ever wander around with aimless sense thinking, "This can't be all that's in this life for me"? The fact is this life isn't just for you! This life is for Him, our Father in Heaven. Your purpose is for Him and this life is to be lived for Him alone. If you are missing God, your life tends to get confusing and you feel misplaced.

In God, we have the promise of a divine exchange. We receive an exchange of precious beauty from God and He takes our ashes (see Isa 61:3). He removes all the dirt from our lives and we simply receive beauty because God loves each and every one of His children. It cannot be fulfilled in any way other than to simply receive the beauty He gives. We can't achieve it, and we don't even deserve it, we just accept it. This is why Jesus died on the cross for us. Jesus' shed blood makes us able to freely receive what God offers in glory, because we are unworthy without Christ. When we fully understand all we need to do to get His glory and beauty is to believe in Him and receive it, we are on our way to fullness and healing with Jesus Christ. What a divine offer!

When we freely receive what He gives, it sheds light onto how beautiful we are in His sight. We are blameless and beautiful, all because one Man, Jesus Christ, died to replace our unworthiness unto God. We have a High Priest, a Savior, who understands and knows our pains because He has gone through the greatest suffering of all. This makes Him able to always relate to us and offer us understanding with peace that provides a comfort the human mind can't comprehend. We are all freely given the option to come to Him and rest in His peace while He carries us and fights our battles for us. He is always interceding for us, pleading with our Father on our behalf (Ro 8:34).

Jesus loved us so much that He died for sinners. He became friends with sinners and showed a love that we can't comprehend. My prayer for you is that you will come to know the kind of love that Christ has for you, and that you will have peace in Him through all your trials. Remember that all things are possible with God. God can do exceedingly above all that we ask or imagine, and he does so with great abundance. When you feel hopeless or when a tragedy strikes your life, God is holding you up and keeping you breathing. He will always be there cradling you in His arms, even when you don't feel him near. He is the One who will never leave you or let you alone. He will wipe away your tears, listen to your pain and joys, always be by your side to hear personally every word, and feel the heartache you feel. He is an all knowing God who constantly wants the best for us, no matter what.

God is love. He knows no other way. Come to Him, and He will give you His rest, peace, and joy. Ask Him to fill you up with His Holy Spirit and the love of Jesus Christ. Ask Him to let His presence be known to you in His fullness. Believe that He is. Know He is there, and love Him with your whole heart, mind and soul. He desires you to be in relationship with Jesus so you may have the best life possible here and eternally in His heavenly kingdom. Let it be known you are not ashamed of our God. Stand up and fight the good fight of faith. He desires to lavish His love upon you and give you the best, to give you the secret desires of your heart. He knows you so well and pays attention to every detail. He cares about your dreams, your fears, and your hang ups. His love for you is great. Seek Him, go after, and pursue Him with all your heart and the rest will fall into place. Simply receive your beauty for ashes.

# Chapter 16

# The Land of the Free

By day and night God never sleeps nor slumbers (Ps 121:3-4). No task is too big or small for Him to give account to and to handle. He watches over us day and night, continuously. Within each day is a fresh, new breath of a life to be taken by the hand. There is a life to be grabbed onto each day, one of continuous cleansing to the state of purity by our Lord and Healer, Jesus Christ. Each morning we wake we partake in a new day, cleansed by the blood of Jesus, and we're given a fresh new start. Every day we have a new beginning all because Jesus died for us on the cross and shed His precious blood for every single one of us. When we take hold of the day He has given us as a gift, we can accomplish great things with the strength of Jesus within us. This requires us to take hold of it, to step out and receive what God has pre-planned for us. Sometimes we have a clear sign something is right and that step is correct, but sometimes we won't have a clue what God is saying. Our place is to seek Him first and joyfully step out in faith with action to find out what it is we are called to do.

We can step out into a place of freedom because we have freely been given the right to be an heir of Christ, put in place by our Father God. What does freedom mean to you? Jesus died so that by walking in His faith and love we may have true righteous freedom. We were not meant to be slaves to anyone or anything other than the One, Jesus Christ, in whom we can trust. Jesus gives us freedom, and because we learn to love Him so much, we can trust Him enough to grab onto His hand and all that He has laid out before us. We trust Him, go after Him, and know that whatever He asks or requires is for our own good. We can trust that He will never harm us, and He is our shield of protection. We can trust that as His "slaves" we will be led to the freedom we each individually seek in our own life.

Whatever it is that holds you back from glory, the pain can be broken by Jesus Christ. He was, is, and always will be, the only One who can free us of our bondage and pain. He brings light to areas of torment. He heals the wounded places in our hearts. He fills our souls with overflowing love that cannot be described. The things that we once loved, we now hate, and the things we once hated, we now love (see 2 Co 5:17). There is no other answer than the prudence of Jesus Christ.

We can fulfill the emptiness in our hearts because we have the privilege of knowing Him and an open invitation to follow and serve Him. We have the unending privilege of serving a Master so great that at His name every knee should bend, every head should bow, and every ear should hearken (Ro 14:11). He is the Almighty God. He loves us so much, He gave His all in blood so that we may be free from our own prisons, and we may know this love in our own hearts. When God knows we are ready for this, true freedom begins. He takes hold of our hearts and works in us until we reach His righteousness, which is at work until the day Jesus comes to take us to His Kingdom, to Heaven where boundless love and copious joy exist.

# Chapter 17

# The Righteous Kingdom

If we walk in the obedience of God the Father rather than in our own will and strength, a new place of holiness opens up for us. We are released into a Kingdom reigned by Him that is pure, holy, and righteous. When we no longer seek to satisfy the desires of our flesh (meaning ourselves), we learn to live the way God wants us to live, in the realm of His Kingdom. All things begin to clear and make way when God is on our side. When we choose to see into His spiritual world of love, the earthly world and views begin to fade. We can start to do things with the boldness and courage we never dared to embark upon before. God helps us every step of the way when it is something He wants for us to do. Remember, we have a purpose and it is not for ourselves. He has our plans laid out before us in His Kingdom, but we must work with Him as a partner to conquer the quest and receive the glory He offers us.

We can do nothing in our own strength. If there is something you have been trying to do and it's not working, or you are feeling frustrated, take a step back, only this time review your situation with the eyes of God. This time ask for His guidance by the Holy Spirit, along with His wisdom and knowledge, since He always has the all-knowing eye of what we can't see. When we step away from our own wishes for a moment it helps us to review our path. When you want God's help, He will help you. As with anything in life, if you don't really want to be helped, no one can help you, not even God. When you allow Him to help you with whatever it is you are seeking, then and only then can He begin to work. At times, it is in a moment of desperation or turmoil that we call out and He rescues. It is only when we cease our own control and give the control over to Him that things will start to look up. Sometimes this may mean doing what you don't feel like doing. Then wholeness can begin. When we rest in Him, God goes to work, and you will find a peace that surpasses all understanding.

If you follow your deep down conscience with wisdom to the depth of your heart, Jesus is there waiting to lead and guide you into love and peace in every situation. Giving up control will not always be easy. For some, it may be the hardest thing to ever have to face. You may feel you always need to have answers but God doesn't always give clear answers. He will help us to break this habit. God doesn't always give clear answers because He wants us to trust Him and seek Him above all else, not just seek Him for the help and answers. He wants a relationship with every one of us, including you! He desires for you to know Him and trust Him wholeheartedly to be able to come to Him for all things, at all times, in righteous prayer.

Pray consistently. That simply means talking to Him and taking everything to Him with reverence. Be yourself and engage Him with respect. There will be times you talk, and there will be times you listen. When you listen, He wants your next step to be obedience because He is trying to guide you to the best life you can have here on earth, even if it doesn't make sense at the time.

We are to serve Him on earth, in love, because Jesus died for us. Even if you were the only one on earth, He still would have died for you on that cross. He still would have chosen you above all His suffering. When we serve God, we aren't doing it to earn any favor from Him, but only out of pure love that comes from Jesus, in us. We then, as a bonus, build up our homes in heaven by all the good we have done for others during our time here on earth. By loving and serving others, we become love, serving Jesus. One of Jesus' commands is to *"love your neighbor as yourself"* (Mt 22:39). This means loving the people around us. We will answer to God in the end of our earthly life and give an account of all that we have done here on earth. We will be judged according to the life we have lived.

The gospel of good works can spread from person to person, bringing light and life into this world if even one person dares enough to follow Jesus. Jesus is God manifested inside each one of us by God's Holy Spirit. Will you be that godly difference in someone's life?

# Chapter 18

# The Beginning of the End

When you reach a place of wholeness in Christ no words can describe the feeling within. When this wholeness happens, we can reach a place of rest, an eternal rest that no one can steal away. When you learn who you are in Christ, you are one of the most powerful people alive. You will have an inner knowledge that nothing else matters except the beauty inside you that is sealed, and made complete by knowing the Son of God.

When Jesus teaches us who He is and we get an inner knowing, an inner revelation of what that means for us as Christians, these feelings surpass any earthly feeling we could ever describe. To reach a place of friendship with Christ will be the beginning of a new life and an end to the old life. He will change your heart through His love for you, and He will show you the glory that can be yours. Often, this is missing for many people, both believers and unbelievers. This is noted by a feeling of void in our lives and an emptiness that can never be filled no matter what we try to do.

The big hole of loneliness, despair, grief, turmoil, or unsettledness is always waiting to be filled with one thing – that one thing is the love of Jesus Christ. He waits for us to receive it. He will never force Himself upon us because He wants us to want to be in relationship with Him. He wants us to invite Him in, all we need to do is ask; this is where the healing begins. This is where there is an end, and a completely new beginning.

Everything will start to fall into place and make sense. Your dreams will become reality. God gives us the dreams we desire in our hearts. He wishes for us to pursue them. Often, a great number of people do not fulfill their destiny because they believe it's too hard or they're not good enough. This is deception by the enemy, Satan, because he hopes to destroy our lives and steal the perfect plan God has set before us. God wishes to create and fulfill our dreams. Believe in yourself and believe in God. Follow the dreams of your heart. Ignite the burning flame that lingers in your heart. It's called having a passion and zeal for life. It's daring to go where you're not sure you will succeed, but deep inside you believe. We have one life to live here on earth. We have one chance to make a difference. Many are called, but few are chosen.

Don't sit back and watch life pass you by. Allow God's dream for you to come to pass. Work at it with all your heart as if working for the Lord. When you know you're unstoppable, the only way to fail is to quit. Never give up. Chase your dreams and your goals like there's no tomorrow. You are the only one standing in the way of making the decision to move ahead or to shrink back. God takes no pleasure in the one who shrinks back (Heb 10:38). It doesn't matter if anyone else believes in you, God does, and that's what truly matters.

What's your purpose? You have one. We all do. Don't sit idly by hoping everything will magically work out. Explore the dreams of your heart. Jesus lives there, and He will help you every step of the way. He will let you know what God's will is for you as you step out. As you continue on this path, you will be shown by the Mighty Hand exactly what your purpose is, and you may just find out it's not at all what you expected! Expect the unexpected, and be open to hear God's purpose for your life.

With every end to pain there is a new journey lying ahead. There is a new beginning waiting to be started. The final destination is home, in heaven, where we will finally be made complete in Jesus Christ and whole in God. No more pain, no more suffering or tears, and no sadness (Rev 21:4). When you follow your heart and allow Jesus to take the wheel of your life, your desires will be fulfilled and a happiness you never thought possible is in store for you! Leave a beautiful legacy that shows Christ's love.

# Chapter 19

# In Conclusion, Take Hold

Jesus said those who put their hand to the plow, and look back, are not fit for service in the Kingdom of God (Lk 9:62). When we live our lives looking backward, there is no room for growth. There is only room for pain and limitations. Jesus advises His followers to continually keep moving forward and looking to the future, even though we cannot specifically see what God has planned. We must keep our eyes ahead, keep putting one foot in front the other, and stop looking back. As we make up our minds to do so, God is there. We are called to put one foot in front of the other in confidence and keep taking step after step forward. As we do, God leads and directs. He is not beside us, He is always before us, leading and guiding our steps into the glory of each individual's laid out plans.

We will not always know the exact path, but God does. We cannot always see what will be, but God does. When we let Him be our saving grace instead of taking care of ourselves alone, we will become the new glory in Jesus Christ we are called to be. Leave a legacy, not just a story.

With God, all things are possible. Until you believe this you will not be able to fully step out and become the person God created you to be. His promises are there all throughout the Bible for us to take. It is up to us to believe them and receive them. We must be put into action in order to receive the crown of glory that lies in store for us. We must work hand in hand and step in step with God to fulfill our God given, blood bought right by Jesus Christ. This is the only way to fulfill our beautiful destiny.

Do you have the characteristics to do so, to be this bold and courageous person? Yes! In Christ, we all do. We cannot do things in our own strength, but with God, we can possess the great land. We can live out all the promises in the Bible. They are for you! If you are not yet familiar with all God offers, your first step is to start reading the Bible for yourself. If you have trouble making sense of it, ask God to help you learn and give you the desire to study by the power of His Holy Spirit. We only learn God's wisdom through the Holy Spirit working in us and teaching us, so keep asking for God to help you. If you really desire to learn and read His word, He will help you. If you find yourself not feeling like reading the Bible, that doesn't mean there is something wrong with you. Simply ask God to give you the desire and to help you.

He wants to help you personally in every way imaginable. He desires the best life for you. God loves you! Believe, and if whatever you believe is God's will for you, you will receive. As you pray, He will continue to conform the words of your prayers into His will. Confess your faith out loud. Start speaking goodness over your life so God hears it, you hear it, and the devil will hear it too. Satan will hear you proclaim your faith in God, and that gives you power and authority over him.

Take hold of the life God has given you today by the death of His Son, Jesus Christ. Life is short here on Earth. Don't let it pass you by and miss out on opportunities and blessings God has planned for you. Seek Him first and all these things shall be added unto you (Mt 6:33). Don't wait another day. Time is precious and so are you. You are God's precious, unique, individual creation, so why not embrace it? Embrace the goodness of you and see all that you are in the eyes of Christ. In His eyes, by His blood, you are perfect.

Give and it shall be given to you. Jesus describes that in good measure, pressed down, shaken together and running over, our needs will be fulfilled by God (Lk 6:38). God is the source of all giving. Give your heart to Him and He will give you the secret desires of your heart. Through Him, watch your life soar!

# Part II

## *Don't Be Mad at God-*
### *Your Personal Path to Healing*

# Chapter 1

# Take Responsibility

My guess is that many of you reading this book have some form of anger towards God. I'm going to abruptly say, do not fall into that trap. It is a trap because it will hinder your intimacy with God, and keep you feeling at a distance from Him. It will hinder your full experience in daily living with the Holy Spirit and God's loving-kindness. We have all struggled with this in some way and at some time in our lives. Maybe now you're asking the question, "Is God mad at me?"

The answer is no! We also do not have a right to be mad at God. We are divinely created, fearfully and wonderfully made (Ps 139:14). Why would God create beings to be in a hostile or bitter relationship with? He wouldn't, and so your challenge begins. Here is where your mental attitude shift must take place in believing that you don't deserve to be mad at God, nor is He the *reason* for the problems you may currently be experiencing.

I can assure you, you have been drawn to this book for a reason. It is likely God has led you to this book because He is trying to bring you to some form of healing in your life and re-establish an intimate connection with you. Something for you maybe is just not quite right, and as humans, we have a tendency at times to push responsibility off on others. This is a big mistake when it comes to the process of healing and will act as an anti-catalyst to the process.

Because sin in this world is running rampant, we all have places in our deepest most inner part of us called our soul that God desires to heal because He is the Great Physician in our lives. But we must submit and allow Him to work.

If you haven't put this book down yet out of frustration, congratulations! You are probably ready to begin your journey of healing, but this time, with Jesus as your personal Healer. When we let down our defenses in submission to the One we can trust forevermore, we can begin a healing process like never before. First and most important in this process is to stop blaming God, come to Him with openness and honesty, and allow Him full access to your heart. When He speaks, listen. Whatever is said is for your own good. If you sometimes have trouble hearing from Him, you're not alone. First, get quiet. Take some time alone with Him where there are no disturbances and you can sit in a calm and quiet atmosphere. Nothing disrupts your time with God more than chaos and noise. You will not be able to hear from Him in the midst of these things. Maybe you will hear a calming voice inside you, or you may get a gentle knowing that you are positive of an answer you seek. Whatever way God reaches out to you, it will always be gentle and peaceful. It will not be harsh, sharp, or hard-pressing. God promises we will know His voice because we are His flock, or simply His children (Jn 10:27-30). His children are in Him, as a part of Him, and we have the wonderful blessing of being able to hear from Him at any time and any place.

God seeks to heal us and love us, and promises to never leave us (Dt 31:8). Do not walk away from Him. He gives us a free will. If you feel far from Him, it is because you have a barrier, something that is blocking you from the full intimacy of God the Father. It can be a form of intentional or unintentional disobedience. Taking time to read the Bible is important because He will bring light to what is hindering you. It is possible you already know you are doing something that is against the will of God, such as holding onto anger or bitterness against someone for example. We like to justify our "right" to feeling certain emotions, but God's Word does not leave room for exceptions. God is clear to give us the instructions He wills for us to follow, not for Him, but for our own good, so we can live the life Jesus died for us to have in joy. Disobeying the clear instruction we find in the Bible is the most obvious way we will be hindered in relationship with Him. He desires a deep, intimate relationship with every one of us. He doesn't pick and choose who to be in relationship with. He is no respecter of persons and does not show favoritism (Ro 2:11). He loves one just as much as the next.

Healing is one of His number one goals because He is a God of justice and does not want us to suffer. We will only ever be completely healed if we allow Him to enter fully into our lives and let Him do the work that needs to be done. The fullness of His glory can then start to be completely experienced in our lives. His outpouring love is for every individual on planet Earth. The path of healing is intertwined with how we respond to Him, listen, and be obedient to His voice, by the help of the Holy Spirit.

In this journey to healing, remember, He only does what is best for us. This does not mean we will never feel pain or go through pain, but if we aren't supernaturally healed from something, He is right there with us at all times, walking us through it so that if and when we go through the fire of life we won't get burned and harbor scars forever. We can be free if we want to be. Is God speaking to you and you haven't been paying attention to Him? I encourage you, now is the time. If He led you to this book, follow and be guided by the Holy Spirit of God, and make the decision that it is time to break free of the personal prison you are living in. Make the decision to stop being mad at God.

# Chapter 2

# Brokenness

B rokenness comes from an unclean heart. It lives in the pain of a heart that has never healed. We may seek but never find. The answers we continually seek can only be found in the One who lives and reigns in love, the Great Healer and the Physician. Our bondage will remain in us as long as we harbor the bitterness and resentment of feelings left untreated. The sting and pain of the emotions we feel from deep seeded wounds will never cease unless we offer them up to God to fix and to care for, and to provide the healing we all crave. We desire an intimate affection that can only be found by seeking the One of true love, our Father in heaven.

Inside each of us there is desire to break free of the pain that lingers inside the heart. It may not always be clear what our hurts and wounds come from, or the extent of the problem, but we are innately created human beings who can feel a heart that isn't quite right.

Circumstances in our lives form us and make us who we are. Our personalities are created before birth but our life situations persuade and develop the person inside of us. If we don't learn to control it, it will control us. It is imperative we learn the good news that we have the ability to take control of ourselves, our minds, and our actions. *"Trust in the Lord with all your heart and lean not on your own understanding; in all your ways submit to Him, and He will make your paths straight"* (Pr 3:5-6).

We can be free of the blind spots Satan has created in our lives but it requires submitting to the Creator, listening to His voice, and being called into action to stop being self-focused. To help ourselves break the cycle of being self-focused, we can move into action by getting busy helping someone else. With the Holy Spirit's power living inside of us, we can do all things through Christ who strengthens us (Php 4:13).

Putting a barrier between our souls and God is exactly what the enemy tries to do by creating a wall so large that we can't break through it. However, when we turn the pain over to Jesus the healing can begin and the walls can be broken down, chiseled piece by piece until we are free. We can then have an understanding great enough to go out into the world and shine the light on someone else who needs God's healing hand of divine help. When we stop trying to do everything on our own and fix ourselves, God can begin to work. God cannot work when we are trying to do what only He can do.

Romans 14:23 (KJV) states *"whatsoever is not of faith is sin."* Remember, if we do not put our faith in God to help us, heal us, and guide us, we are not trusting in Him. God works through our faith and our trust in Him. When we are lacking faith God is not pleased, even if it's a small area in our life. All things require our faith to be put in Him. Trust Him to do the healing. Trust Jesus to come into your heart, heal the wound of the soul, and declare freedom over your pain and bondage. It will take time and consistent effort, but you will start to live the life of freedom God has called you to have in Him!

# Chapter 3

# Wholeness

Celestial beings create a habit of personal intimacy. Jesus is the Truth. When we come to truly know Him and have a personal relationship with Him in intimacy, He will begin to set us free of emotional pain and bondages that have been consistently holding us back. It is true freedom once Jesus works in our lives and we can experience an unleashing of the harsh pains relapsing on the inside of our soul.

Jesus came so we could be free. Figure out what freedom means to you personally. Write it down, declare it, and speak it over your life. What you hear yourself say is what you will start to believe. For example, if you are a "worrier," declare war against the state of worry. Let's go back to Romans 14:23; whatsoever is not of faith is sin. Therefore, if we are in a constant state of worry we are not fully trusting God, and have some form of doubt that He is in control. Worry is a feeling, an emotion we must learn to control. Jesus did not live in a state of worry, and He is our living example of completeness. He trusted His Father that all things work out for good to those who are called according to His purpose, and love God (Ro 8:28). He knew every day was filled with the love of His God. We also have this love at all times as God's children.

When we remain in a constant state of worry, doubt, disbelief, or confusion, to name a few, we are letting our emotions rule us rather than trusting in our sovereign Lord. God works through faith so we need to be living in faith at all times. It will not always come easy, but resting in Jesus creates a lasting peace where we no longer have to fear the unknown. His righteousness takes away the sin of the world; our sins, and we can rest and rejoice in that.

We have been called according to His purpose, so it is of great importance that we find our place of greatest intimacy with God. When we get quiet long enough to listen and spend time with Him we can begin to know His wants, His desires for us, and even know how He feels about the way we are living our lives. Born-again believers should live a life full of passion to serve the One who loved us first. When He is first on our list the rest falls into place. When we seek God and not other things or people of this world to satisfy our desires for happiness, life becomes highly enjoyable. There is a purpose, zeal, and a passion only God can reveal. When we call out, God shows up! He waits until we truly want Him in our lives and He's right there waiting to wrap us in His arms.

Unconditional love is felt from deep within the heart. Many times our souls are pierced with a love that is conditional, based on our performance or how we act as individuals from childhood into adulthood. The love of Jesus Christ is not so. His love is an unconditional love offered to all of us as sinners, for forgiveness and to teach us we are deeply, inexpressibly, loved by Him, no matter what we've done. We can be reconciled to Him and to God by receiving the free, unconditional love He offers. It cannot be found anywhere else but in His open, out-stretched hand. We all have the offer. Will you receive the fullness of it today?

Painful wounds deep in the midst of the soul often are left unhealed and pushed back. They are left suppressed and forgotten, yet our subconscious does not forget. It lingers like an infection in our bodies that can never heal unless we make the decision to face the pain and let Jesus heal it. We cannot heal the wounds ourselves. We are not capable to take away the pain in our souls that was created by others either intentionally or unintentionally, whether you were five, 20, 50, or older. Pain does not go away if it is left unhealed. We can try to patch it or run to things for comfort, but it will still come back to manifest in us in some other way if we don't deal with the pain and emotional wounds. Wounds cut deep. Therefore, they need time to be dealt with and brought to the surface. The process will usually not happen quickly, but the freedom that follows is well worth the wait and effort. Love yourself enough to open up to yourself and get quiet with you. Spend quiet time alone, not multi-tasking or doing other things; spend time with just you and stop running from the pain. Remember, God wants to heal you and give you a life of freedom. He never brings evil upon us, only acceptance and love. He may not always take us down an easy path, but He knows the healing will allow us to be all He has called us to be!

# Chapter 4

# Pushing Past the Pain

O ne of the greatest lessons to be learned is that hurting people hurt other people. When we as humans are wounded emotionally on the inside, many times it comes out in wounding another person unintentionally. We must remember that God is not the author of pain. He does not cause bad things to happen to us. Bad things happen as a result of human sin and disobedience to God. It is easy to get caught up in the enemy's trap thinking that God is punishing us or that He is mad at us. The belief is then created that God is unjust and that He is making bad things happen to us. Nothing could be further from the truth because God wants only *good* for His children. The walk with Jesus is not always easy but we have the promise as followers of Christ that all things will work together for good for those called according to His purpose.

As God's children we have been given a plethora of promises all throughout the Bible. As we seek Him and trust Him He will reveal these promises to us in scripture and throughout our everyday walk with Him. God never causes anything to happen for our harm that will not work out for good, so wipe that lie clean off the slate of your mind in this moment. We can trust Him with ourselves and our lives more than we can even trust ourselves. How do we do that? By faith; faith is trusting in what we currently cannot see or do not know the answer to. Faith is trust in God that no matter what the outside circumstances look like, He will prevail and give us beauty for ashes. Faith is a deep-knowing that God will work all things together for our good in His perfect timing.

Maybe you have been hurt and learned never to trust people. God is sovereign. He is the One who we can always put our faith in, lean on, and He will never leave us, nor forsake us (Dt 31:8). He has given us mercy and grace even as sinners, to be redeemed to Jesus Christ. That alone should tell us we can trust Him with our whole heart. This takes time, and if you will be faithful to Him in your life, He will always be faithful to you, but He cannot work in a closed off heart. He cannot breathe life into a heart that's cold and bitter, and refuses to turn to Him. When we learn to give our hearts to Him, He reaches down and begins to work in whatever areas we need work. He is love and only knows how to give love.

God, faith, and trust all go hand in hand. They work simultaneously to bring us a new, fresh life deep within our souls and a peace that surpasses our own understanding. We as human sinners are the issue at hand, not God. God is perfect and in Christ, we are seen as perfect also because He loved us first. We cannot bear bad fruit (such as holding on to being mad at God) and expect Him to bless our lives. When we follow His ways, we will then bear good fruit and be the example of Him we are supposed to be. Believe and receive the greatness and healing He has planned for you today!

# Chapter 5

# The Author of Beauty

Frustration sets in when we are not following the will of God. It is easy to believe that we have our plans made and figured out, but if they are our plans and not God's plans, it will not be a smooth ride. God calls us for His purpose, not our own and if we aren't following His path we can become confused, frustrated, and easily distracted. The enemy can deceive us at this time, to think God doesn't love us or that it is all God's fault our lives are miserable. In reality, sometimes we need to get quiet, be still and listen. We must listen for God's leading and guiding.

When we are in His will things are much easier, flowing at a pace of ease and without struggle. It may not be easy, but things always work when you are in the will of God. His plans are always better than our own because He sees what we cannot. He has our safety and our own best interests at heart. God surpasses our own understanding, so we must trust by faith that He knows exactly what He's doing at exactly the right time. Believers must learn to walk by faith consistently. We cannot please God without our faith (Heb 11:6). This strong faith comes from Jesus Christ, who gives us the ability to believe. We are nothing in our own strength, but in Him we are more than conquerors! We are always equipped to exceed and be victorious because Jesus goes before us and is always there to help and guide us. He never leaves and we must lean on Him completely. We need to be dependent on God alone not ourselves, or anyone, nor anything but Him.

Complete and total dependency also comes by walking in faith. Those who believe will learn to live without doubt no matter what the circumstance, when it agrees with God's word or His will. We cannot make up our own rules, but we can freely live by God's grace, mercy, and love. In doing so, we can live life with ease and a complete reliance on Him because we trust Him. Trust comes by spending time with Him and getting to know Him intimately. This does not mean going to church once a week and forgetting about Him for the rest of the week. We cannot expect to have an intimate relationship with Him without seeking Him on a continual, constant basis. A meaningful relationship is two sided and we will reap what we sow. If you feel distant from God, check the time you are dedicating to being with Him in prayer, studying His Word, and meditating on His true love for you. He does not keep us at a distance. He seeks to be close with us, so we must always be in check with the effort we are putting into our relationship with Him. He loves us but it also requires us to make the effort to set aside time to grow with Him. When you seek Him with your *whole* heart, you shall find Him (Dt 4:29).

In this life, we will have trouble. We must realize that does not mean God causes it. Many seem to be mad at God, believing that He is the author of chaos and distress in life. First and foremost, we must know that we cannot understand God fully but we know He always wants what is best for us because He loves us. He knows what He is doing, even when we don't. That is why we must believe in faith and not lean to our own understanding, and simply trust. Trust that He is always good and He is a God of love (for study see 1 Jn 4:8-10).

Because sin entered into the world long ago by the sin of Adam and Eve in the garden, Jesus said that we are to expect that in this world there will be trouble. Yet, we will not be overcome by it because God is always fighting for us as long as we trust Him and keep our faith in Him. He will never leave us or forsake us, and He is not the author of evil things, only good. Jesus taught in Luke 13:4, that certain things beyond our control are just a part of life in the world. We are not to get bitter and blame God. It is easy to put a label on a tragedy and get mad at God for it. Real faith humbly accepts that we live in a fallen world, and that Satan also has great power.

Our enemy, Satan, tries to destroy anyone who will allow it. The type of faith we are given as believers also realizes that God is only good. God is our shield and protection, the lifter of our heads. He is always there to help us and raise us up, but God can only work through our level of faith. He longs to give us beauty for ashes and to care for His children, which is all of us. He loves all of us the same. He will bring positive light and life out of every circumstance if we look to Him, trust Him, and ask for His help. He knows our pain and listens to our cry. He comes near to us in our times of need and He is there in times when everything seems to be just fine. Although, we must listen and be obedient to His voice at *all* times, not just when we need help. We must know by faith and His word that He has our best interests in mind. He seeks to heal, bring peace, joy, and happiness. God is good; He is not the author of bad and evil things.

# Chapter 6

# The Seemingly Impossible

I n this world you will have trials and tribulations, the good and the bad. But regardless of the ups and downs in this life, on the top of our mental list must be our next life to come, with the richness of cheer and treasures. There will be no lows and there will be no evil. All the waves of sin will be no more. So let me ask you this question: *Where is your main focus?* Is it on God and our new life in Jesus Christ in heaven, or is it here on earth and earthly things? One thing is for sure, when your mind and heart are continually on earth rather than God and heaven above, you will fall apart. Life will make you bitter and angry, and inside you will feel broken in pieces. During these times we find ourselves stressed out and overwhelmed, looking for things or other people to make us feel happy and satisfied, but never feeling at rest. We cannot extinguish the longing feeling for something to keep us happy. The only thing that will cease this unrestful longing is Jesus Christ, and when our eyes do not stay *continually* on Him, we leave the door open for the enemy to work discontentment and anger into our hearts. "*For where your treasure is, there your heart will be also*" (Mt 6: 21). This means that whatever you focus your mind on, this is where your heart will lie, whether good or evil. If you give the enemy a foothold, he will create a stronghold. So

I urge you to honestly ask and answer for yourself this question: *Am I mad at God?*

Quite often we must get quiet, be still, and take the time to search our souls. The enemy is very good at deceiving us and making our thinking very misconstrued, blaming God or other people for things we need to take personal responsibility for. Until you "own it", confess it and take responsibility for whatever it is you are harboring in your heart, it will stay there and you will continue to be deceived, broken, and torn. God created us to be in an intimate relationship with him, not to be bitter and resentful towards Him. He is for us, not against us, so we must first set one thing in our minds straight, and that is God is ALWAYS fighting for us and never against us. That doesn't mean He will never discipline us, but it is always out of love. We must stop blaming God for our messes and take responsibility for our actions.

God is the Author of peace and all good, not confusion or evil. If you find yourself questioning God often, your first priority must become to learn the beautiful character of God by studying His Word and spending regular time with Him, not just one day a week on Sunday. He created us for fellowship. *Fellowship* means companionship, relationship, and partnership (Merriam-Webster Dictionary). God teaches us how to have intimacy with Him by His Holy Spirit if we desire and seek to have that type of connection. A relationship is not one-sided. What you put into a relationship is what you will get out of it.

Once you truly know who He is and become aware of His beautiful character there will be no need to doubt the goodness He has planned for you. He never does anything to vindictively harm us; getting to know Him and His character will promptly reveal to you that you have no need to be mad at God because He is for you in *all* things. If something unpleasant is taking place in your life right now, remember that God will always work all things out for good if you believe in Him and trust Him in the midst of your situation. Be thankful to Him that He is working on your behalf, and He will, in His proper timing, work it all out for good no matter how impossible it seems at the time. One of the most beautiful verses in the Bible is, *"Jesus looked at them and said, 'With man this is impossible, but with God all things are possible"* (Mt 19:26). What do you believe? If your belief is in God for your breakthrough and for His supernatural help, He can work in your situation, but if you are full of doubt and unbelief He cannot work. That is why we are called "Believers," not unbelievers. Once you know God's true and unchanging character, you will start to be able to discern by the power of the Holy Spirit, the good works of God.

We have the opportunity to make decisions and to make the choice for our minds to line up with God's Word or with the enemy. In a similar sense, this can be compared to positive and negative. We know having a positive outlook in life tends to yield positive results in time, just as trusting and believing in God will yield His best for us. We must remain in this positive place full of hope, no matter what it looks like on the outside. We never have to go it alone. We can ask for God's help to keep us strengthened and uplifted. When He sees us trying to remain thankful even when things look bad in the natural, He is right there to pick us up, help us, and is very happy to do so. He loves us in faithfulness with an everlasting love that cannot be separated from Him.

When you give your best, God gives His best, but He will not do everything for you. We must make an effort to do what He is asking us to do, as strong, firm believers, and not weak, pitiful, unbelieving people.

# Chapter 7

# Crucifixion Becomes Personal

"*Greater love has no one than this: to lay down one's life for one's friends*" (Jn 15:13). It is plain to see the love God has for us. God came down from heaven, became flesh as Jesus Christ, and took on human form to die for us on the cross. Jesus gave up His own life so that we may have life and be reconciled to God in love. How many people do you know that would give up their life for you without even thinking twice? And this was not just a death, but a crucifixion; a painful, slow, torturous death to save us, people who are sinners. We were lost but became found when Jesus made the decision to be obedient to God and accept death on the cross to save our souls. This shows God's love for us. This shows He would not want anything but goodness and happiness in our lives. He is always on our side.

It is easy to doubt at times God is with us or for us, because in this world we see so much destruction and devastation, and go through serious situations of hurt and despair. However, God promises that He will be right in the midst of our pain in every situation and never leave us. He promises to wipe away every tear and to keep us lifted up in confidence, carrying us through all of our heartaches. He is never the cause of the heartaches, but He helps us with His loving hand to get through it all and come out on the other side stronger, having learned something. This means gaining godly wisdom and in turn, then being able to go forth and help someone else in need.

When we are hurting the best thing to do is put ourselves aside and seek to go help someone else. It gets the mind off of our own problems and brings a smile to our face because we are showing God's love to others. Seek righteousness and love, not self-pity and hatred. You don't have to do it alone. God will help you. It is easy to place blame and pass on the responsibility to everyone else. One important lesson that Jesus taught is that we must not be hypocrites. By definition, a hypocrite is someone who claims or pretends to have certain beliefs about what is right but who behaves in a way that disagrees with those beliefs (Merriam-Webster Dictionary). He teaches we must be careful not to be so judgmental or critical of others that we fail to see our own wrong doings or shortcomings (for study see Mt 7:1-5).

Many times we do this without even realizing we are being critical towards someone for something, while we are doing the same type of thing, or even worse. It is an evil set up that keeps us in the trap of failing to help ourselves and others. We are to always look inside ourselves and pay attention to our inner self first before we try to speak to someone else about their faults. What would the world be like if rather than judging others we chose to give them a compliment, and chose to love instead of being critical? We can be so focused on what someone else is doing that we don't like, we can neglect to see our own issues that God is trying to deal with us about.

Jesus many times spoke harshly to certain people and specifically, the group of Pharisees, "You hypocrites!" This is because they were deceived in believing that they were pretty close to perfect in their own actions by living up to the standard of the law but failing to use the action that is most important to God: love. When we open our own hearts to God and ready ourselves to let Him reveal things to us, He will show us our own faults and weaknesses because He is trying to create the best version of us we can be by creating godly character within us. Be careful in all things not to be blinded by your own self-identified perfection, that you miss out on the wisdom God is trying to give you to create the ultimate character of beauty within you. It all starts with becoming humble enough to take time to look at yourself and honestly review who you are on the inside and how you treat others regularly.

We all have a conscience and that conscience comes from God, His Spirit. So when we let this Spirit-led conscience guide us in God's wisdom, we almost always instinctively know what's right. God teaches us every step of the way until the completion and coming of Jesus Christ, but we must allow Him to do the work He needs to do within us. If you are not willing to be humble and to submit yourself to His loving authority, He cannot work in you to the capacity He desires. Hence, it is not His fault if you hold a rebellious attitude. Yet, He loves us so much that even if you have pushed Him away and now you are ready to submit, He has been waiting for you. He loves you so much that He waits for our own stubborn pride to move out of the way and to return back to Him. He waits with open arms to invite us back to Him as He draws us near.

# Chapter 8

# Justice for All

I believe living a truly born again, resurrected life means taking into ourselves the identity of Jesus Christ and becoming one flesh with the Father, just as we associate ourselves with our earthly family bloodline. We must remember first and foremost, God is our family bloodline. He is our Father and we are His children. We are one in Spirit with Him. If we deny our "oneness" we lose a lot that He has to offer us. We can unintentionally deny His goodness because we may not take hold of all that He lays before us by His free gift of love and grace. To be one with represents unity, in the image of, and the likeness of, so to God we are seen just as He sees His Son, Jesus Christ if we dare to believe it and receive that free gift by faith. But, it is our part to reach out by faith and take hold of this image.

Second Corinthians 5:17 (NLT) states, "anyone who belongs to Christ has become a new person," so no matter what we looked like before in our "old" self, our "old" physical and spiritual selves, we are new and born again. We are new and born again spiritually, from above by God's Spirit. God offers His glorious love to every person and we have the beauty to simply come to Him and receive it. So then, if He so freely offers this great gift, why would He do things to hurt us or intentionally make our lives miserable? He would not and He cannot because God is love. It is foolish to believe that God is the source of anything in our lives but ultimate good. He is always for us and never against us in His ultimate purpose. If you have problems believing in this area, the goodness of God, then please study God's character diligently. When you truly know who God is you will never question in your spirit His character and great works.

Just like any loving, adoring, parental figure, He will seek to be the lifter of your head and work all things out for good no matter how ridiculous our failures have been in our lives. He is for us in all things and constantly works on our behalf. We can trust Him with our entire being, our lives, and all that we are. The trust we are to put in God cannot be compared to trust on earth like with other human beings. We are human and we will never be perfect but God is, and He will never let us down. It begins with trust; trust in Him and His character.

Many times people question God about the injustice that happens in this fallen world. Number one, we are living in a fallen world that does co-exist with personal enemies and evil spirits that seek to tear us down. Number two, the Bible tells us God is not the source of any evil. Sometimes it is easier to get mad about injustice than it is to trust God with it. This requires great faith in Him and perseverance in faith without ever giving up our hope in whatever it is we are believing for, as long as it is in line with God's will. We can't expect Him to bless us for selfish reasons and then get mad at Him when He doesn't answer our prayers. We cannot act like immature children in this area. We need to be spiritually mature in faith, hope, trust, and perseverance. They are all linked and no force of evil can stop this, if we have our trust in God.

God also works on things behind the scenes. Just because we cannot physically see that He is working, we must believe that He is and that maybe it's not exactly what we are praying for, but to know that whatever He decides to give us is indeed the best thing for us. God is a sovereign God. He is a ruler over all things in love. He reminds us in His Word to be ceaseless in prayer. Therefore, that keeps a direct connection open with Him at all times. Prayer is simply talking to Him about everything. We don't need to act all types of holy when we speak to Him. We need to approach Him with respect and reverence but be relaxed and comfortable. At first, this may feel awkward to you, hearing that you can be relaxed when speaking to God, but He wants us to be. He doesn't want us to be afraid of Him. He is a loving God and a loving Father who dearly loves His children. He enjoys our fellowship and relationship with Him, and we are to go to Him boldly with a courageous attitude and offer ourselves as His prized children. We are co-heirs with Jesus Christ (Ro 8:17) and we may rest in that fact alone because Jesus is and was perfect. When we go to God as His child, He sees us like He sees His own begotten Son, Jesus. One of the most amazing things about our God is that He sees us like our Savior!

We are to always be ready and waiting for God to answer our faith prayers. Sometimes this will call us into being active and doing something out of obedience and sometimes it will require us to just wait patiently for Him to move. We can rest in the fact that God will act as He desires for us to act and this means He will overcome all evil with good in one way or another (see Ro 12:21). We can be reassured our sense of feeling an injustice comes from God because He created our innermost being. This means

He feels our pains and wounds, but we must be patient and give Him time to work in our situations. At times, He may just say, "Be still" or simply, "Wait for Me." We will not always know what He is doing or how He is going to do it, but we must know that He is working for us and not against us. There are countless times in the Bible where the people trusted God even when everything seemed wrong, later followed by God's deliverance of answers and goodness out of His pure love for them. This places a guarantee in our hearts that He will do the same for us.

It is important during the bad times (and of course good times); even when we are hurting or all seems dim, that we continue to praise Him and thank Him for working and for all He does for us. We cannot get bitter and angry and let it fester. However, there are times we will have these feelings because we are human, but by the help of Jesus and the Holy Spirit, we do not need to remain bitter and angry. If we are true followers of Jesus Christ then we must do what Jesus would do in all situations to the best of our ability, with His help, and that just may mean a sacrifice. It definitely means surrendering your own emotions to Jesus no matter how you feel and do what is right by trusting God for justice and vindication in everything.

# Chapter 9

# Have you done your part?

D o you seek God diligently? Is He the first or last part to your day? Are you aware of Him and speak to Him throughout the day? I believe many Christians don't have the fulfilling life with God they could have because we so often do not put in the time to reap what God offers. God does not just offer physical gifts and blessings. He also always offers such wonderful gifts as love, joy, peace, patience, kindness, goodness, faithfulness, gentleness, and self-control (Gal 5:22-23). He gives every believer the same opportunity to have an intimate relationship with Him.

So why does it seem some people are closer to God than others? It is definitely not because God plays favorites. The Bible tells us God is no respecter of persons which means He treats us all the same, with the same love. Many things in life greatly depend on the time we as individuals, are willing to put into fellowshipping with Him in worship and studying His Word. We cannot expect to be close with Him or have the life He has called for each of us to have if we are not spending personal, quality time with Him and listening to Him in return. This also requires obedience to His voice and promptings. A spiritually mature Christian will seek to do what is necessary first and foremost, more importantly than anything else in their day, to spend time with Him and gain personal intimacy, even if it is only in one minute time frames. This is because of the personal realization of how important and valuable time with God is in our everyday life.

God honors our trying with our whole heart. When we seek to give God our time, He will give us the time we seek in return, which will make the way for a more peaceful schedule. Everyone has been given 24 hours per day. Each of us must choose how we spend it. We are the only one responsible for our schedules. God must be first, not last, and when He is first, everything else will fall into place and ultimately work how it's supposed to. We cannot expect to give God our last minutes of the day after we have checked everything else off the list and have our lives be filled to completeness, in abundance, the way God offers it.

What is important to you, you will make time for. Now you must sincerely ask and answer for yourself this question: Is God most important to me in my life? Before you answer, take a personal look into your days and note how much time you give Him, and take note of the quality of that time. Do you watch the clock to fulfill the set standard you have for yourself in devotions and praying, or read a chapter of the Bible so you can get your reading accomplished for the day? Or, do you devote undistracted, cherished time to your Creator? What you put in, you will get out of the relationship. Do not expect God to do all the work. He will do His part when you also do your part. Consistent, diligent, devoted action produces a fruit with God that cannot come from anything or anyone else.

We as Christians also have to be careful not to fall into the trap of becoming so busy doing things for others that we never take our own personal time with God. It is a beautiful thing to help others and do as much as we can for the service of God's work, but we can get caught up in doing so many "good works," that it takes all our time away from our personal, undivided attention with just ourselves and God. We can be our best and do our best if we are spending regular fellowship time with God because He grants us that strength to go out into the world. We are to have a heart of service, but we are not to let it overtake spending time in prayer, studying the Word, and seeking to know God more intimately on a personal level all the time. More than anything, He desires a relationship with us and for us to deeply know Him. Don't let your good works and being so busy *"working"* for God take over that you forget to take time *with* God.

## Chapter 10

# Knowing God

God's righteous characteristics are never changing. People change, but God does not (Mal 3:6). He is the same yesterday as He is light years from now. He is good, patient, sovereign, and long suffering towards us. We are to model His character and to be the resemblance of Jesus. If more people would act like Jesus with a highest standard of morals and integrity, the world would become a different place. If everyone chose to love instead of hate, we could all come together instead of pull apart.

Lack of knowledge of God's character and His Word is a huge problem, and learning it is extremely important and valuable to us as human beings. If we live in ignorance of the proper way to live, and choose our standards over God's standards, we will surely not have the righteous, abundant life God calls for us to have. We cannot live by our emotions and how we feel. They will almost always lead us astray. A spiritually mature Christian will abide by God's standards, not by the ever changing guidance of feelings. The problem is that if the Word of God is not studied and put into action consistently, it cannot work.

*"My people are destroyed from lack of knowledge."* (Hosea 4:6)

The lack of knowledge of God and His character is an issue that we can address and take responsibility for. Again, what is important to you, you will make time for. Knowing God's character is one of the most important and valuable things a person can ever possess. By knowing Him, we can learn to trust Him and rely on Him completely because we know He is always for us. Knowing God deeply, allows us to relax and to come to Him with all things, opening up for us a new way to live.

Knowing what the Word of God says is also very critical to live the amazing life God has planned for you. It is the key and the instructions to life. It is the wisdom we need to live day to day to the fullest, with joy and an understanding of the prosperity of God. God's prosperity can mean blessings, health, financial abundance, happiness, family, friends, and the list goes on. When we trust Him and rely on Him because we know He will never cause us any evil harm, we can go to Him boldly and accept His gracious love and abundance in Jesus Christ.

There is a difference between reading the Word and studying the Word. We need to study the Bible and anywhere the Word can be found, not just read through it to accomplish the task. To truly study the scripture allows us to take it into ourselves, to tuck it in our hearts, and have revelation of what the words of the pages mean for us and our salvation. Jesus is the Word made flesh, so He brings the words to life in us. He speaks to us through these words, but He can only do so if we allow it and believe it. He won't fully work or bring revelation where there is unbelief.

A problem area for many is unbelief, even for born again Christians. Read again Romans 14:23; "*whatsoever is not of faith is sin.*" I think it is very safe to say unbelief is a sin. It shows we are not trusting God in some way. Remember, Jesus Himself said, *"With man this is impossible, but with God all things are possible"* (Mt 19:26). All we need is the faith of a small mustard seed and God can and will work through that to bring about His purpose. This gives Him the opportunity to work in our lives and show us His great power and majesty. This doesn't mean we can ask God for anything and everything we desire, but if it is in the will of God, we can be sure He will fulfill it as our desires line up with His, if we only ask and believe.

> *"Ask and it will be given to you; seek and you will find; knock and the door will be opened to you. For everyone who asks receives; the one who seeks finds; and to the one who knocks, the door will be opened."* (Matthew 7:7-8)

# Chapter 11

# Compassion for Christ

When we come to the realization that Jesus Christ has died for us personally we can live with a greater sense of value. We can accept that even if the earth was only dwelled upon by you, Christ would still have made the decision to give His life for only you. This is hard to grasp and comprehend when on earth we live a life of great affliction. Why would anyone do this for us? This Great Spirit that lives and reigns in heaven is all around us. This promise and gift of life is offered to all because of a great love. God's love is never changing and never fails. Since we are of human flesh, we cannot identify fully with Jesus' actions of love. We simply are called to accept His love and not try to figure it out. We can rest in the simple satisfaction that He loves us, so we can receive it and have the great life He has called for us to have. No love like this will be found on earth. It is this type of love that we seek, but will not find except through Jesus Christ. It is by choice whether we accept or deny His free offer of love.

God looks at us with the eyes of love. Our love is not the same as God's love, but we can progressively be turned into a character more like Him because Jesus has come to help us. When we receive Jesus, we have full access to God our Father with closeness, boldness, and courage. We are to be strong and mighty in Him, not weak, powerless, and pitiful.

It is important that we understand Jesus' character to begin to perceive God's love. Jesus made a decision to be obedient to God and God's plan. He would surrender His life and be put to death on a cross, to be crucified by nails driven through His body. Have you ever imagined yourself receiving this crucifixion and in addition, doing this for people who may not even know who you are or do not like you? Prior to His death on the cross, He chose to receive the whipping and lashings cutting deeply into His flesh, with great amounts of blood running down His skin. He accepted His cross while people watched, laughed, and mocked Him with jeers and insults. Continue to see yourself in His position. You do not open your mouth to fight back with words. You take it all upon yourself because you made a decision to be the sacrifice God needed to save mankind and to love people instead of letting them suffer for their own sins. A crown of thorns, inches thick, was shoved into His head as blood ran down His face. All the while, He could have chosen to end it at any time. Why didn't He? Jesus is LOVE. He made this sacrifice, for you, so that you may come to know Him, and God, so that you may know this intimate love He offers. Because of Jesus' actions, we do not have to suffer an eternity in hell of fire. Yet this is only a glimpse of His suffering.

We do not know what it means to truly suffer. As followers, we love Him because He loved us first. We are all equal and He chose us first. While He was on the cross suffering until death, you were on His mind. He chose you.

Thankfulness and gratitude of the heart will not come until we can fully receive and acknowledge what He did on that day.

He gave up His own life so you might have life (see Jn 3:16-17). He gave His all so you may live and enjoy your life. As we receive this offering, we will begin to fully respect Him by being grateful and living for Him. We are free to live with gratitude every day of our lives and enjoy every breath we take. We are here in this time because of Him, not by chance. Our lives were chosen and put into action by one decision: *love.*

# Chapter 12

## Sedentary, an excuse

G od is love but without your personal acceptance of His love (that is Jesus Christ), and personal redemption, His love cannot manifest inside of you. Our life on this earth is a journey destined to be fulfilled with God's one and only Love, by His plan. We must learn to seek Him and trust Him to walk it out in the physical. As we learn to trust Him and His guidance, we will see His good plans put into action through us.

Action is a term of movement. We must not be sedentary if we want to be used by God and help others. Some tasks are large, others are small deeds, but all are important to God and none are lesser of value. We are all members of the Body of Christ, called for His purpose. We each have a place and a purpose to fulfill as part of the body. Some are called to great missions in the world, others are called to be stay at home mom's with a deep, loving care for their families. Whatever it is you are good at, and being led in your heart to pursue, go after it. Don't just sit back and do nothing. *"Whatever you do, work at it with all your heart, as if working for the Lord, (not for human masters). It is the Lord Christ you are serving"* (Col 3:23-24). We are called to live a life of excellence and happiness, which means a life we truly enjoy. We were not created to be miserable or live a miserable life. We were created to be joyful and worship the Lord, and in return, receive the beauty God has pre-ordained for us.

To put ourselves into action requires first that we listen. Listening to the voice of God requires peace and a willing heart. Peace requires sometimes getting quiet so we can hear from God. Busyness can often create distraction, and then we cannot hear from Him. The U.S. is one of the busiest places on Earth and it is good not to be a sluggard, but there is a large difference between busyness and productivity. God-inspired action leads to productivity, not busyness. Being continually sedentary is an excuse not to be physically, spiritually, and mentally put into action for the Lord. He cannot work through a lazy heart.

Often times there may not be a huge desire in our heart to feel like doing something God has asked us to do to help someone else, but our call to action is to listen and be obedient when in your heart you know the task has been set before you. If you are being led to do something, it could quite possibly also be part of God's plan that He is trying to get you to take part in something in order to bless you. Set yourself into action so that you will also be rewarded or receive a breakthrough by your obedience. He may be trying to set you up for His reward to you, not because you deserve it by action or works, but because we eventually reap what we sow. We cannot live a segregated, miserable life and expect to be blessed by God. Being sedentary rooted in laziness is an excuse not to do something. We must take action and move to the good plans God has for us. We must take responsibility to do what we are called to do, whether large or small, and trust God whether it makes sense to us or not. Fear may attack, but we are not to let ungodly feelings control us. Many emotions may attack us, but we are not to let them run our lives. They are not an indicator of how to live. God is the only true guidance we have and we can trust. He gives us His guidance and love by the Holy Spirit.

It is a good idea to create a time of peace and quiet for yourself on a regular basis without distraction so you can hear what He may be speaking to your heart. Many of you are thinking right now, "But I don't have time, my schedule is too busy." In reality, you are saying you don't have time for God. You are telling God, the Creator of the universe and the One who has given you life that you do not have time for Him. This obviously is not the right choice. Keep making the mental note, what is important to me, I will make time for, and there is nothing or no one that is more important than God. Setting a schedule of priorities, and setting these priorities in proper order is very important to you living a blessed, peaceful, joyful life. When God is first, everything else will fall into order and you will see things change for the good without struggling to make things happen on your own.

As you put God first, even if it's only a few minutes to start per day, you will find He will honor that, and He will help you fix your schedule to proper order. He will create more free time and peace for your enjoyment. Ask Him to help. We are not to be so bogged down in life that we forget what's important. Don't be mad at God because of the life and schedule you created. Ask and it shall be given to you, in accordance with God's beautiful will for you!

# Chapter 13

# Hasten the Way

Different personalities are led by God in different ways. The way we respond to God can highly depend on our individual God-given personalities. Some people are naturally bolder while others are more shy and timid. Some people may have an identity that seeks to stand out, while others are more comfortable to sit back and be part of the crowd. Whatever your personality may be, none is right or wrong, yet we must be careful not to ever use that as an excuse not to change if need be, or to treat people wrongly. We are to use our personality characteristics the way God wants us to use them.

As you begin to follow God, He may call you out of the crowd or He may ask you to be a follower of someone else He has chosen to be a leader. When we listen and step into the role He has called us to, the process will work beautifully, but if we fight to play a role He has not called us into, it will become a mess. We have to become skilled at paying close attention to where we are called to be and what role we are called to play in life, and then step into that role. This will require character and a humble attitude. For example, if you desire to stand out and be the leader in a situation but you know God is telling you to step back and let someone else be the leader, maybe in a Bible study or a position at work, how will you react and respond to His instruction? Will you submit and do what's right according to God's will or do what you feel like doing? It is always wise to look ahead. Wisdom says in this case, "God is saying one thing, yet I feel like doing another, but I know that God is asking this role of me for a reason so I will follow." Whatever the reason may be, when God asks us to do something, we can trust it must be the best way for us because this is what He chooses. The rule here is simple: if we do it our way, the end result will be a mess. If we do it God's way, everything will work out for good.

So often we follow our own opinions and ideas and do not seek God's. This is foolish in many ways but simple for the fact that He can see what we cannot, so we can't simply rely on self. He sees the big picture, and we only see a glimpse. We can only see the now, and so often our minds are clouded. What we think we can see or understand may still not be right for us. When you learn to follow the leadership of the Holy Spirit, life flows in a much simpler, more peaceful manner, and we can relax in knowing that God has everything under control.

He has a beautiful heart and we must continually thank Him for His love and care. We like when other people appreciate us and the things we do, and God is the same. When He does stuff for us He appreciates our praise, worship, and acknowledgement. Praise Him all the days of your life (see Ps 34:1). Do not be overbearing and impatient. When we seek to do things our way, even if it is the right way, if we aren't in sync with God's timing, the outcome will still be a mess. God has a will and a perfect timing for everything and every person. It's not our way or timing, it's His, and whether we decide to listen or not, one way or another

He will work it out in His manner because He ultimately has the almighty power and control in love. Make a decision today to break free from the trap of choosing your own path and choose the divine path of our Almighty Father.

# Chapter 14

# An Identity Rooted in Christ

A personal identity is how you see yourself. If you come from a life filled with abuse or turmoil, mostly likely you may be suffering from a disturbed sense of self, unless you have unleashed it to our great Physician, Jesus Christ, for healing. The first step to healing is admitting and surrendering. We all must come to a place where we individually utter from our own mouths the truth of the trauma we have suffered. Our childhood affects our being and the first step is to speak your pain and speak the trauma. Unless you recognize it and declare it happened, you cannot break free from it.

It is easy to live in a place of denial. Here, the pain of truth doesn't have to be accepted as our own life, but staying trapped in it is even harder. Denying the life God is offering is much more painful than releasing the guilt and/ or shame that hides itself in the soul. Present your requests to God. With His help, whatever your personal healing request is, He hears you and will begin the moment you surrender it to Him to allow Him to do the work He needs to do in you. This promotes inner healing. He will always finish the work in you (see Php 1:6) He starts because He desires our joy and happiness. He desires our pain be completely removed and healed.

Many of these inner pains are hidden away in our hearts, without even knowing they are there. Seek God first above all else in life, and He will reveal things at just the perfect time and heal what needs healing. We cannot fix or heal ourselves. We must release our wounds into His hands and let Him do the work. The direct connection to God is Jesus and unless you have a personal relationship with Jesus, healing will not take place. God cannot work in you if you don't surrender and give way to His Son, our Savior and Lord Jesus Christ. When you accept Him and ask Him for help, He will make His home in your heart by the power of the Holy Spirit and the process can begin. His goal for us is to be more like Him and to love Him by serving Him first and foremost. This will lead to the life He has in store for us.

Our lives will not always be perfect, but God's perfect will can be worked out in us. Cast down your own self, your own waves of sin, and He will continually cleanse you of unrighteousness. He will show each and every one of us the way. If you don't give up the reigns of control on your own hurt and pain, He cannot lead the way. He can't work when you are still trying to be in control of your own life and self. We serve one Master and that is the God-head, Jesus Christ. We cannot serve ourselves or anything else and still whole-heartedly serve God. We must seek Him first and all else shall be given unto you (Mt 6:33).

When we become reliant and focused on our Master God, we can quickly fall into the place He wants us to be for our own personal good. We start to become the person He has set before us. We can start to release bitterness, rage, shame, guilt, feelings of rejection and abandonment, and be the unique person we were created to be. We no longer are held back by emotional feelings linked to our past hurts. We are newly created and linked to a new creature; an identity directly connected to Jesus Christ.

When we become this creature of Jesus Christ and accept Him as our personal Savior, we are no longer our own being. We are now seen by God like His own Son when He looks at us. He sees Jesus as He looks upon us. This allows us to be bold, courageous, and proud in a godly way, the way God calls for us. He is always guiding us and making us more like His Son, but we must allow it and let Him in. When you seek, you shall find. *"Ask and it will be given to you; seek and you will find; knock and the door will be opened to you"* (Mt 7:7). Is Jesus knocking on the door of your heart today? Have you let Him in? Stop hiding in your pain. Seek it, release it, and let Jesus heal it. He cannot work in a shut-down heart. You must allow yourself to go "there," to feel the pain, anger, grief, and heartache, because when you open that door to Jesus, He will heal it, and you will not face it alone. Don't bury it any longer. If you're not sure what's in there, seek God to let Jesus show you. By the Holy Spirit, He will reveal it and bind up your broken heart of old wounds.

You may be pondering if this will really work for you. Yes! His Word, the Word of God, promises all of this healing, and it works! It has worked in my life and many others around me. It will work in yours too. What have you got to lose? Stay in your pain, or give it to Jesus and watch Him work. *"The Lord Himself goes before you and will be with you; He will never leave you nor forsake you. Do not be afraid; do not be discouraged"* (Dt 31: 8).

# Chapter 15

# Your Personal Path to Healing

Are you mad at God because of what you have suffered in your life? Maybe you have shied away or run from Him because of your feelings of hostility and anger towards Him. He is a *just* (fair) God. He does not cause evil things to happen to us. Sin entered into the world starting with Adam and Eve (see Genesis). Adam and Eve disobeyed God after receiving clear direction from Him in the Garden of Eden. Because of one human, sin entered the world and has brought calamity upon Earth, but by one Man, our Savior Jesus Christ, He has removed our sins and seeks to bring us wholeness in life. When we suffer tragedy, many times our first result is to blame others for our trials. This is a bad habit we must not follow, and blaming God is not the answer. First and foremost in character, He is a God of love, a God of justice, peace, and harmony.

As we come into an intimate relationship with God, you will at all times know by faith that nothing He directly does to us will bring or cause us harm. He does not know sin in His heart, only love. Therefore, we can trust Him. If you have a problem trusting because of past hurts, know that at all times, you can trust God. He is not like people. We are mere human beings, living in a fleshly world, but God is not of flesh. He is a God of Spirit and great love. He is always in control so that nothing that happens to us can overtake us. When you trust Him, it allows relaxation and peace, which brings happiness of heart no matter what is going on around you, because you can know that God will take care of you. We get ourselves into trouble at times because of our worldly attitudes of unbelief. We live by our emotions and circumstances rather than the Word of God. Keeping our eyes on Him allows us to have an inner knowing that God is in control and we can rest safely in His arms, knowing that nothing shall ever harm us outside of His protection (see Ps 91:9-11).

When we trust, He can work and we can rest. We can rest knowing that whatever happens, He will work all things out for our own good (see Ro 8:28). When you trust Him, in some way, all things Satan means for our harm, God will use for good because God is all-powerful. We must stop blaming everything on God and use wisdom. We must know that there are differences between God, the works of the evil one, and natural calamities for example. If we are in a state of constant blaming and anger instead of trusting in God, all things cannot work out for good because this keeps us in the trap of not being able to release the emotions that hold us in bondage. This is not trusting and believing in His goodness. When you change your mindset from bitter to trusting His sovereignty in all things, you will notice a change in your life. But this starts with you.

Make a decision today to come to Him, repent of your sins, repent for not trusting Him totally, and begin again. He is waiting to be good to you. Make a decision to trust Him no matter what the situation looks like or what you have been through, and you will see your life begin to change. All things take time so it cannot be a one-time situation of trust. It must be a continual affirmation in all things, "I trust you Lord. I believe you are working all things for good." Peace will be right around the corner for you. Remember, God does not force you into anything. You must make a committed decision to seek, trust, and love Him.

## Chapter 16

# Be Thankful

T rials can make us bitter, resentful, and full of hurt. Let me remind you of a very important verse that can change the way you feel immediately: *"Rejoice always, pray continually, give thanks in all circumstances; for this is God's will for you in Christ Jesus"* (1 Th 5:16-18). We are told to do three things. Number one, rejoice always. We need to keep a right heart by continuing to rejoice in the storm, no matter what comes our way. We are to keep praising our God because we can trust Him. We can trust that whatever happens, He is holding us up and will work it out for our personal good.

Number two, pray continually. This is a clear command to pray without ceasing, no matter what feelings stand in our way. Praying continually simply means conversing with God at all times. This doesn't need to be in a certain place with quiet time, but to be in a constant state of fellowship with Him so you are talking to Him all throughout your day. He wants to be a consistent part of your day and life, not just sometimes or only when you need help. Continual prayer also consists of seeking Him all day long by knowing He is there and thanking Him for it.

Number three, give thanks in all circumstances. By trusting God, we know we can yield a continual feast of giving thanks to

God because we know He is good. We trust in Him and for Him to work out all things in accordance with His perfect will, and we know His will is always the best thing for us. Remember to look at the big picture, not just the now. Sometimes things may appear to be bad when actually God is going to use that very thing to turn it around and use it in some way for your own personal good. If you do not trust Him, He cannot work. Therefore most important for you in all situations is to remember to consistently trust Him no matter what the outside looks like. Trusting in Him through all things, good and seemingly bad, opens the door for God to work in our lives.

Faith without good works is dead (see Jas 2:17). So then, one of our good works is to put into action getting our minds off ourselves and helping someone else that may be hurting, rather than dwelling in self-pity and allowing this type of pity to take over our lives. Helping other hurting people will create a sense of joy on the inside of you that will help soothe your soul while you wait for God to work on your situation. This will also set you up for a reward because you are following God's desire for you to help others. If you are hurting, ask God, "How can I go help somebody else?" What you sow will return back to you. Love others and you will find a new love for your times of trouble. When we are weak, God is strong for us (see 2 Co 12:9).

# Chapter 17

# Cease Your Anger

Fellowship with the Lord is crucial to your success in this life. Jesus made it clear, without Him we are nothing and can do nothing (see Jn 15:5). Without recognizing Him in our lives we will never feel fulfilled and reach the life we dream. Many times we reach out, feeling starved for something in our souls because we are empty due to our own transgressions and sin, yet when we let go and let God, that empty space starts to fill with the love and every single thing we have been missing. The empty space or the void of darkness begins to gleam with a new light never known before. When we allow Christ to be the center, the Lifter of our head, our pain ceases despite our circumstances. The darkness of the circumstances of our lives is nothing compared to the peace and joy Christ brings. He makes it seem that all the darkness just fades away.

When two, Christ and self, become one, Christ as the Head and the Leader, there is a heavenly peace that surpasses all understanding (see Php 4:7). This type of peace can only come from God. When you truly know God, know who He is, and share an intimate relationship with Him more than just knowing of Him, the reverential fear and awe we have for Him will drive us into an even closer fellowship with Him. Remember, don't be mad at God. He is an easy target for us to be mad at because we want somewhere to place blame for mishaps in our lives. What we should be doing is partnering with Him to find our greatness. We can find out exactly the beautiful plans He has for us. Do not be mad at God. He is the only one who can help you and guide you into total happiness. You must be on the same side with Him, ever-increasing your intimate fellowship with Him.

God is the glorious Father of all creation and calls each of us to fulfill the beautiful destiny He has pre-planned for every single individual. When we partner with Him, instead of being angry at Him, our lives will begin to bring joy no matter what the circumstance. We will find good in all things because we trust Him and are led by His Holy Spirit, not our own physical minds. He sees what we can't, so one of the biggest, most important roles as Christians is to believe and trust God, no matter what the circumstances look like. He is always working behind the scenes. Even when it looks or feels like nothing is happening, He is working. He is the Author and Finisher (Heb 12:2 KJV) of life. It would make sense to believe then that He has everything under control and nothing is too large in scale for Him. We must trust. Seek Him and let the joy of the Lord be your strength. Be content and satisfied in all situations (for study see Php 4:11-13). It is your choice.

It is not the circumstances that form us, but our reaction to the circumstances. You've heard the saying, "When the going get tough, the tough get going." This can also be known as having perseverance and never giving up. True faith in God means never quitting. It means pulling your shoe strings tighter and stepping forward, staying in sync with God. When He moves, you move.

Keep paying attention to the feeling in your gut, the gentle promptings or knowing's deep down inside. The devil will try to feed you the lie that you don't hear from God. He will whisper to you and make you think, "Other people hear from God, why can't I?" Stop this thought right in its tracks. It is a lie; it is not true. God speaks to all of us in different ways, we just need to take undistracted quiet time to get to know His voice, and in time, it will become easier to recognize it. We all have the ability to hear from God because God loves all of us the same. One example is our conscience. He speaks to us by the gentle prompting in your gut, guiding you every day. He is always speaking to us, leading and guiding us to the best, but we have to pay attention. Not our will, but God's will be done.

To be confident means trusting in Him, not ourselves. He is always gently leading and guiding us but if we are not peaceful and we are filled with wrong emotions, such as bitterness, resentment, anger, or rage for example, we cannot fully hear from Him. Who are you mad at? Maybe it's not just God. Maybe it's a person you feel you can't forgive. Feeling these emotions isn't wrong; it's letting your emotions control you that become the wrong action. We cannot live a Spirit filled life led by God, and hear clearly from God, if we are not putting into practice what God teaches us in His Word of the Bible. We cannot harbor these feelings with an unforgiving spirit towards God or anybody for a lengthy amount of time and expect to have intimacy with our heavenly Father; it blocks our ability to have a right relationship with God. We can easily start to make a bigger mess in our lives because we are not being obedient to Him on a command so clear in His Word. We leave the door open for the enemy in our lives if we are not obedient to follow what we know is right in our hearts. Deep down we know holding grudges or being angry is not something we should hold on to, yet as humans, we so often choose to do it anyway. This creates disobedience and opens the door for the enemy to gain a foothold in our lives which can easily start us on the path to blame God for things.

Many of our own messes in life can be eliminated if we are obedient to the Word of God and His promptings. If you feel you aren't hearing from God, be still and get quiet. Spend quiet time with Him without distractions. Make the time. Do not waste another day making the excuse, "I don't have time." Otherwise you are telling God, "I don't have time for you, Lord. Other things in my life are more important than you." You don't need to sit down for hours at a time if you don't have that kind of time. If God sees that you are making an effort in your busy schedule to give Him at least five minutes, He will reward you by revealing His wisdom to you. This time with God is the single most important thing in your life. If you don't spend time with Him, you will never truly know Him, and therefore, will not fully have the great life Jesus died for you to have. What is important to you, you will make priority time for- this goes for anything in life. Whatever you spend time on, that is what is most important to you.

An excuse is a reason not to do something. Start going to God with a willing heart, and He will start to reveal Himself to you once He is the priority in your life. Many are called, few are chosen (Mt 22:14 KJV). He is waiting for those who respond to His call. The first step is to be still, get quiet, and listen with your heart.

*"Anyone who listens to the word but does not do what it says is like someone who looks at his face in a mirror, and after looking at himself, goes away and immediately forgets what he looks like. But whoever looks intently into the perfect law that gives freedom, and continues in it- not forgetting what they have heard, but doing it- they will be blessed in what they do"* (Jas 1: 23-25). Own up to your own disobedience; if that is the root cause of your anger toward God, confess it, let it go without feeling guilty, and God will forgive by your asking with a true heart. Don't waste another day being mad at God and having a distant relationship with Him, wondering why nothing seems to be working out for you. Seek Him today, go after Him, and start a brand new relationship of intimacy with Him!

God is so patient and loving; He waits for His children (each of us) to listen, to be obedient to His Word, and to want to do what is right; we can only do this with His help. This opens the door for God to act instead of the enemy. Choose life. Choose God, our gracious heavenly Father and seek His ways. You will live a life of *"beauty instead of ashes, the oil of joy instead of mourning, and a garment of praise instead of a spirit of despair"* (Isa 61:3).

# Part III

## *The High Life-*
*Increasing the beauty of your destiny*

---

# Chapter 1

---

# A Higher Road

Perhaps you picked this book because you want to learn how to create a better life for yourself, to live the life of your dreams. Perhaps you have it all mapped out in your head, what your "perfect" life would be. Don't be discouraged when I say that you cannot create your perfect life. You cannot achieve the perfect life of happiness. There is a large difference between you working for something, or by learning how to ask for it and letting God freely give it to you by His loving grace. If it is His perfect will for you, then you will receive what you ask for. *"You do not have because you do not ask God"* (Jas 4:2). God is a gracious God who desires to lavish His gifts upon His children. We do not need to fight or struggle to get them, we simply receive them by His giving right hand (a free act of love He offers) as He shows us how to work at the things He calls for us to do.

When we let go and let God do things His way, our lives become richer and sweeter. We no longer need to struggle to achieve the life we desire to have if we are working at the tasks He calls for us to do. He gives us what we need, when we need it, and this is one of His beautiful promises in scripture (see Php 4:19). He cares even for each and every bird of the sky and feeds them; will He not care for all His children even more? (For study

117

see Lk 12:22-26.) God will see to it we are well taken care of in the ways that we need if we trust Him.

This promise is not saying that some of us will never struggle with lack of some good thing, or that we are to be sluggards in life. We may even have to go completely without things at some point in life, to grow and to learn in our faith. We can't answer why we all must go through our own hardships and situations other than we live in a sinful, fallen universe since the beginning of our creation. The one thing we are required to do through all of this is to trust Him. If we keep our minds in a state of belief in His goodness instead of doubt and remember that God does not cause bad things to happen, we can find a place of rest even during hardships because we trust all things will work together for our good (Ro 8:28). We may learn many things during our times of lack, and in turn, the circumstance can create a deeper intimacy with the Lord; we learn to trust Him even more because we must rely on Him completely to make it through our difficulty.

One thing that is promised is that everyone goes through the same types of hardships. We must be careful not to be deceived into thinking that others we compare our lives to are not suffering in their own ways. This creates a self-pity mentality and leads to a place of further sadness and anger. God always holds us up but we can easily bring ourselves right back down if we are not careful what we choose to focus on. We have a choice to make. We can believe God for His good promises to come to pass, or we can believe the spirit of fear of the enemy that we will never make it out of the hard place. If we believe we won't make it, then we are choosing to be miserable. Feeling downcast starts with a beginning place. Where you let your mind go, will be what overtakes the thoughts in your mind. We need to have a clear focus on right things. God reminds us to keep our eyes set on Him and things above, nowhere else (see Col 3: 1-3). If we take our eyes off of Him, we are choosing the eventual path to destruction. Staying focused on Him means believing His truths rather than the downtrodden, depressing thoughts of the enemy's lies.

God says, *"I am the Alpha and the Omega, the First and the Last, the Beginning and the End"* (Rev 22: 13). With God, you can have the end to all your struggles, hardships, and pains because He gives us Jesus Christ as the sacrifice. You must choose life over death, joy over sorrow, sun instead of rain. Calling to Jesus will help you do this and you will be a victor, not a victim.

# Chapter 2

# Resurrection Power of Jesus

When you believe in your heart that you can achieve great things, you will ultimately end up doing great things. Your mind is a powerful tool that has the ability to hurt you or harm you. You get to choose how to use it. We have all been given the freedom of choice. By learning to control the mind's thoughts and use it for good you will be taken to higher levels in life.

*"Do not conform to this world, but be transformed by the renewing of your mind, then you will be able to test and approve what God's will is- His good, pleasing and perfect will."*
(Romans 12:2)

God specifically shows us that we must be aware of taking control of our own thoughts with His help. Through Jesus living in us, our minds and thoughts will begin to change in accordance with God's thoughts, not the defeating thoughts of this world. This happens if we choose to meditate on God's Word and not our emotions. He will never leave us to do this on our own but we do have to make the consistent, conscious effort to conform to His Truth. We should never leave our minds idle to think about just anything because this leaves an open ground of emptiness to be used by the enemy. He will dump his harmful thoughts into our minds. The Bible clearly warns us to *"be alert and of sober mind. Your enemy the devil prowls around like a roaring lion looking for someone to devour"* (1 Pe 5:8). Satan will not miss out on an opportunity to harm the one who doesn't pay attention.

Being of noble character doesn't require us to be perfect. It requires that we do our best, so that God can then give us His best. A sluggish attitude of negativity and grief cannot be used by God because it is not focused on God. Where you direct your focus is critical. What you focus on will become larger in your mind, for the good or the bad. Whether you choose the high road or the low road is up to you. God gives and chooses His best for every one of us but we must learn to walk in step with Him to receive it. We must learn to live by His guidance, His words, and to use our faith to fulfill the life that we are given. Jesus gave His life for us to have the best life we can possibly imagine. He didn't die for us to have a miserable, unfulfilling life. When you seek Him and keep your eyes focused on Him, you will in due time reap the wonderful life God has chosen for you.

*"Peace I leave with you; My [own] peace I now give and bequeath to you. Not as the world gives do I give to you. Do not let your hearts be troubled, neither let them be afraid. [Stop allowing yourselves to be agitated and disturbed; and do not permit yourselves to be fearful and intimidated and cowardly and unsettled]."* (Jn 14:27 AMP) This is a call to action of our minds and our free will to make a choice to use Jesus' power to follow Him. When we make the decision and effort to be a victor over our minds, God will work and continue working until the end of our days on earth.

# Chapter 3

# Seek Him First

Putting one foot in front of the other every single day and going out into the world requires keeping a great faith, whether intentional or unintentional, in mind. This faith in our hearts and minds should be focused on one thing: Jesus Christ. When we are solely focused on Him, our days become shorter with grief and longer with joy. Faith is given to those who ask for it. James 4:2 reminds us, *"You do not have because you do not ask God."* We may remember to pray about large things overtaking our lives, but it is essential to remember to pray for godly things freely given by God's power. We need to pray for things such as wisdom, strength, authority and power in the Holy Spirit, along with the very important: great faith. One of the biggest challenges in our walk of life can be living without a great faith. It is offered, but we must choose to use it. We must choose to take hold of that of which Christ died for us to have (Php 3:12). If we do not reach out and grab all of that which is offered in Christ, we won't reach life's fullest capacity in our daily walk with God.

Don't compare your gifts or the talents God has given you with someone else. If someone seems to have a greater faith than you, for example, embrace this as an opportunity to ask God to help you and to give you a greater faith by the Holy Spirit. Use the open door to prayer as an opportunity to seek God and ask God for things your heart desires. Then trust Him that He will give you exactly what is right for you. It may not be the exact answer to the words of your prayer, but God works to answer in His timing and His righteous way.

We can make the mistake of becoming whiny and complain that we don't have what others may have. This is a fault we have as humans to seek and want what we don't have because somehow we can feel what we have is not quite good enough, or that there can always be something more, something better. When we learn to be happy and satisfied at exactly the place God has us in our life, He begins to work. This means having a thankful spirit and a thankful heart for all that God does, no matter how big or small. When we reach this contentment in life and spirituality, God will show up, reach down, and begin to move larger in your life.

Remember to ask; offer praise at all times, and then ask with a right heart for what you desire. You are in a place, a time, a season, for a reason. God places us in seasons of our lives to learn something and to bring us closer to Him. Instead of asking, "Why," be asking, "What should I be learning from this, God?" With an open heart and mind on your part, He will show you. He answers those who wait on Him, and in His due season, He will move.

Do not hinder Him from moving in your life by doubt and unbelief. These two things will hold back all the goodness He has in store for you. Keep watch over your heart and mind that you do not leave an open space for the enemy, your adversary, to sneak his way in your heart by wrong thinking and steal all the goodness that God offers. Remember to keep in mind scripture warns us to *"be alert and of sober mind"* (1 Pe 5:8). The devil is always looking for ways to steal our joy. Pursue all that God has to offer you. Don't get stuck in a pit, a place of destruction, forgetting to ask God to show you what desires He has specifically placed in your heart. Go out each day with great faith and guard your heart from the enemy. When you seek God, you will find Him. Be open and willing to watch Him work in many ways each and every single day of your life!

# Chapter 4

# Your Adversary

*"Be alert and of sober mind. Your enemy the devil prowls around like a roaring lion looking for someone to devour."* (1 Peter 5:8)

One of the most important things for a person to learn is that Satan is a real enemy, a real spirit that roams this earth seeking out people to prey upon. His main purpose is to steal everything God offers us to enrich our lives (see Jn 10:10). Satan wants us to be miserable and in pain, so therefore he works his hardest to attack God's people in any way possible. The realization of Satan being a "real" enemy against us, and not some made up creature, is not meant to be scary, but to show us we need to be alert and of sober mind to stand firm in our faith through God. Our instructions are clear not to ignore Satan so that we can work with Jesus to defeat him in all ways; we are also told many times throughout scripture not to fear. We need not fear because Jesus has given us more power and authority over every wicked thing than any enemy of ours possesses (see Lk 10:19).

We are to stand firm, steadfast, and resist Satan with Jesus' authority so he and his wickedness will flee from us. We are God's children so we will always hold more power than the enemy. We must listen also and submit to God so that we know how to respond and work with God when we are under enemy attack. When the devil attacks with his wicked schemes he cannot win against us because we hold inside us the power of the Holy Spirit, God's almighty power. Nothing can defeat this power, and we hold the power freely because we are His children. Whenever anything or anyone comes against us, we need not fear or submit to any sorts of evil because we are God's children. Jesus died for us so we freely and openly have the right to use His Holy Spirit's power in our times of need.

This is not the same power that mankind sometimes craves as authority, but the righteous, loving power God provides because He loves us. We do not have the right to go around telling people what to do or being controlling over others, but rather a power to know that we are children of the Most High God! We are children deeply and richly loved, who by the faith as small as a mustard seed can move mountains (see Mt 17:20). Jesus tells us that God will help us if we only have little faith to believe in Him and believe that He is good. Then, He can help our faith and authority to take hold of that as the apostle Paul said, which Jesus died for us to have in our own lives. Jesus paid a high price for all of us, and we can choose to deny or accept His sacrificial love. When we choose to accept His love, we accept Him, and we accept our God.

Satan cannot prevail over God, and we can remind him of that. We can remind him that his time is coming to an end because God tells us this in the book of Revelation. By taking authority of these words, I believe Satan's power over us as individuals is weakened. We can quote scripture, as Jesus did, and speak the Word out loud. Any time we do this it makes our enemy weaker. He cannot win wherever God is, and God is everywhere. We must follow God by submitting to Him, be eager to follow His ways, and God will lead and guide us in defeating the attacks we face daily by our one true enemy, Satan, the author of all bad things.

Following God is not an option if you truly wish to have the abundant life of blessing Jesus promises us if we abide in Him. Satan tries tirelessly to steal our peace and joy so that we find it very challenging to hear from and follow God. To live the high life with Jesus sometimes means a sacrifice of self to truly love others. Sometimes we won't get treated the way we wish to be treated, but Jesus promises that if we love one another as we love ourselves, that God will be our vindication. We can trust Him to make things work together for good at just the right time. Satan will try to tell you to treat others unfairly or have a hard heart against the world; God does not choose this for us. We have basically two choices to pick from at all times; the high road or the low road, which means God's way or Satan's way. An easy rule to defeat the enemy at all times is to love others, which overcomes Satan's evil. We are to overcome evil with good (Ro 12:21).

As we learn God's character and know how He wants us to act, by reading and studying scripture, we will learn the true ways of God so we can act in obedience and submission to Him; He has our best interest at heart. God is the only One we can trust upon at all times and in all situations. He will never lead us astray, so it is very important to keep our minds clear, free of clutter and chaos, and to be in peace. When we are not in peace and are distracted by busyness of our lives and schedules, our minds become easily taken off God, leading us to stray off course. Our minds alone can work so hard in overdrive that our minds even become too busy. When we are in sync with God, we know in trust by faith we are following the right path. Satan has come to steal us away, kill, and destroy us (Jn 10:10), so we must be in tune, making a conscious effort at all times to pay attention to all things, even our minds. If Satan can to get us off course and be miserable, he will do it.

Remember, God is all powerful so we do not have to let the enemy rule our lives with his negativity and pain. We are children of God so God's power is for us, not against us. We can use His great strength to battle anything in life that tries to get us down, but we must also make the choice to do so. We must make the choice to choose God's way, not the enemy's, or our own. The spirit is willing to follow God but the flesh is weak in our own strength. We can do all things through Christ who strengthens us (Php 4:13). Note the "in Christ"; we cannot do anything in our own strength, alone. Jesus helps us at all times if we ask and look to Him. Our eyes must be on Him at all times or we will fall prey to Satan's evil schemes.

Imagine the colors black and white. Black will represent negativity, Satan's ways, while white will represent God and positivity. By our wisdom, we have proper choices to make: white or black, God or Satan. Let us make wise choices by choosing God's thinking and His ways of life, not the opposition which will make our lives miserable if we allow it. We all have times of trouble but Jesus says to "take heart" because He never leaves us and we can *always* rely on Him (see Jn 16:33).

## Chapter 5

# Think Large

Freedom is something we all have an opportunity to grasp. We can take it or leave it behind. The freedom in which we can possess the great and fulfilling life is ours if we choose to seek God. He gives us the freedom to choose Him over the world. God is not of the world and because of this, we as Christians are asked to live a different lifestyle. When we join our will with God's will and hook into His greatness, we will see great things come to pass. We will see things happen in our lives we cannot imagine because God is good. He is for us and once we learn how to fully trust Him consistently and devotedly, freedom of our souls will start to take place.

Because God asks us to lead a different life than to live like the rest of the world lives, we can be assured that if we follow His commands by His gentle promptings, the small or large sufferings we face will seem smaller and less overpowering to our minds. We can take hold of Christ with resting assurance, rather than take hold and meditate on the problem. Jesus died for our sins, every one of them; past, present, and future so we can freely live by His love, guidance, and understanding (see Jn 3:16-18). We do not have to flounder around just existing in this life until we pass on. He desires for us to live a free, joyful life that surpasses any description in words. He is for us and there is no stopping

His genuine love that is offered to us. We can choose His hand or what the world offers, but when we become true followers and seekers of the Lord, there is great peace that far surpasses our own mental understanding (see Php 4:7).

God is good; He never lets us fall. He always waits for us to seek Him first to really move strongly in the individual life He has given us. One move of His breath in our direction can open up a whole new level of freedom in our soul. If we are faithful to diligently seek Him, He will be faithful to us in ways we cannot imagine. God is a god of the impossible (Mt 19:20). Our minds sometimes prevent Him from doing all He is looking to do for us. He will move mountains in our lives when our faith in Him becomes as large as mountains. When we believe and trust He can and will do miraculous things of beauty in our personal life, He will start to move. Don't limit God by your small thinking.

When we open up to Him in belief and heart, He will show His awesomeness in our lives. He promises beauty for ashes. He knows our hearts and wants to do great things for us. When our minds open, this creates the freedom in our souls in so many ways, each of us getting to experience for ourselves the personal "freedoms" God gives. This could be through revelation (by the Spirit of God) or in the physical realm. Begin to study God's works with the people in the Bible. As you do, open your mind to see that these amazing things are not just for the times of old. We serve the same Almighty God. God is the same; He does not change. His miracles and provisions hold true for anyone who chooses to believe in Him first, not to those who believe in themselves. His miracles are for those who boldly dare to believe God's promises hold true in the now.

# Chapter 6

# Alive in Christ

At times in our lives we come into submission of our own desires and not God's. When we learn to get out of the way of ourselves and let God do His work, we can rest in His peace and find that life becomes easier. We still may go through hardships but we don't become lost in a mountain of our problems. Our problems seem less daunting and overbearing. When we let God be in control rather than controlling our own destiny, He can and will, use our hardships for good. He knows how to teach us in a way that we learn from our mistakes and get to use them for His glory. With God, nothing is ever wasted.

He is glorious and magnificent and when we truly, fully rely on Him, He changes our lives to glorious and magnificent. This happens when we look to Him always and not our circumstances. At the same time, He changes us. He changes us to be so beautiful and glorifying that we are perfect in His eyes. Our faults, our hurts, our wounds, He takes them all and gives us beauty instead. He can transform our lives in ways that we cannot possibly imagine. When we remove God's "limits" in our unbelieving minds, He can begin to work and create in us a masterpiece for His glory.

God works day and night so that we may have rest. We can safely rest in His arms to know that if and when we fall, He is there waiting to pick us back up. It is like a child who is learning to ride bike for the first time. The child may fall as he or she is learning, but Dad is there to pick up His child, brush off the skinned knees, and set the child back upright on their feet. He doesn't ever leave us to fend for ourselves or to be alone. We may feel lonely but we are never truly alone. God is there to pick us up no matter where we have been, no matter how bad we've messed up. He picks us up, brushes off the bruises, and sits us back up to begin again. If we won't limit God, He will be there guiding and leading, and all we have to do is follow with a right heart. He sees what we cannot. It is only wise to trust in Him, not ourselves, at all times.

Scripture tells us to run our own race (Heb 12:1). Sometimes we get caught up in the world trying to run someone else's race, trying to be what they are or achieve what they have achieved. We clearly cannot choose someone else's path or we will never feel satisfied and always feel confused or misled. We need to follow our own path and run our own races. We need to follow the path God has laid out for us, not our fleshly desires. When we focus on God's will, we get the pleasure of running our own race and living our own life with joy. We get to be free of working to be like someone else whom we admire, and we can let go of striving to achieve what we think in our mind is right for us. Where God says to go, we go. When God says move, we move. If God says stay, we stay. Take your mind out of the equation. We don't have to understand everything God says.

If you know in your heart God is telling you something, run with that. Don't turn from this thought or back down from what you know and feel in your heart. Follow your heart (with godly wisdom), which is where God can prompt you to run your own race of life. His plans for you are not ever the same as someone else's. Stop allowing others to run your life for you, and put God in control. When you give Him the control seat, He will walk you down paths you may have never been down or dreamed of. Keep your eyes on God, follow the Spirit's promptings in your heart, and you will find the freedom to live your own life!

# Chapter 7

# The Lost Get Found

Putting off ourselves and our own fleshly desires for God's will sometimes will require a self-sacrifice to be the person God wants us to be and do the things God wants us to do. Jesus lived a life of self-sacrifice to simply love other people, but this was not always an easy task. There were a great many times He was not popular with people, and He was regarded as crazy. Yet, He knew who He was. He held fast to the fact that He was a child of the Most High God. He knew His position of authority not in self, but in God. This allowed Him to freely be a representative of the One true God everywhere He went. He went about doing good to others and loving people.

We are called to do the same: do good and love others. We are also children of the Most High God. We hold the same power and authority because it has been given to us by the blood of Christ; we are in His bloodline (see Ro 8:14-17). We can show this love of Christ if we choose to walk in it. It means showing love even when others don't deserve it or don't treat us kindly in return. First Corinthians 13 talks about all the ways and the traits of love. It shows us that love is not just a feeling. It is a great place to study the characteristics of the love we are called to walk in and show consistently to our fellow neighbors (who are the people all around us). It tells us that even if we can do many astounding things, but we do not have love, we are nothing and will gain nothing.

Showing love to others does not require a special talent. To show love, which preaches the gospel of Christ without having to use words, we aren't required to hold a special title such as Pastor, Bishop, or a similar title. To show the true meaning of the gospel anywhere we go, we can show love by becoming ministers of Christ's love. Love shows the heart of Christianity. Love shows the Truth, which is Jesus Christ. We can preach about Him through our actions, by giving our heartfelt love to those we meet. In doing so, we have the opportunity to show others who our Savior is. Many do not know Jesus, but by bearing His fruit, the fruit of the Holy Spirit: love, joy, peace, forbearance (patience), kindness, goodness, faithfulness, gentleness, and self-control (Gal 5:22), we become a representative. By giving these "gifts" to people we are representing all that Christ stands for. We have the opportunity to win those who are lost, those who do not yet know Jesus Christ, by being the example of His witness. Check in with your own actions. Those who are lost need the guidance of Christians, those who truly represent who Christ is, not just by the title of "Christian". They need to see the actions of Christ being put into effect on a consistent basis, not just when we feel like it. God works through people, meaning us. He uses His people to work in other's lives.

People need an answer other than what they see in the world. The world's ways are Satan's ways, but God's ways are not of the world. God's ways revolve around one thing and that is love. We should be shining examples every day of Christ's love. Because we live in a corrupted world, we must *diligently* seek God for His help. We must ask Him to help us be who He wants us to be, and bare the example of what He wants to show others through us. By seeking God, having a right heart given to us by the Holy Spirit, and making a conscious effort to choose to walk in love, people can be led to Christ by the actions of love we choose to pursue.

# Chapter 8

# Seek The Kingdom

With the Lord and His special anointing, we can do anything we put our minds to within His will. We must learn how to follow God's path for our lives by making a diligent effort to seek Him in our daily lives, not once a week at church or every now and then when we get "free" time. As we put God in first place, doors begin to open and the doors that aren't right for us begin to close. We don't always know what the plan is for our lives but the faith comes when we just trust. We must trust the anointing on our lives to do what we need to do, not just to get by, but to live a joyful, accomplishing life, spreading joy unto others at the same time. If we trust with consistent, un-doubting hope and faith that God's ways are perfect, and therefore follow Him by His Word, we will see many new beautiful things come to pass. We can't expect to make things happen in our own strength, but if we trust our God, His love and guidance will never fail. His righteous leading will continue to be perfect in our lives every single time if we learn how to fully trust Him.

One thing that surely pleases God is that we consistently, unswervingly, put our faith in Christ Jesus. When our eyes are on the Lord, there's no room for anything false to sneak in because we can always reference the Truth in His Word. The deeper we know Him, the more we learn to trust Him, not by our own strength but by making a decision and effort to seek Him with the guidance of the Holy Spirit.

The Holy Spirit knows our ins and outs. He knows us so well that even when we are confused about ourselves and our own minds, He is right there to perfectly lead, guide, and protect. He moves with us and in us at exactly the right time; exactly the moment He knows we are ready for whatever it is God lays upon our hearts. He is gentle, kind, and prompts us into righteousness. God only knows how to love us at all times, so we can never be forsaken by Him and His great love. When we seek our Creator, the One who made us intricately and perfectly, life is full of blessings and opportunities we could never create ourselves. We can let go and let God work, so that we can enjoy all He has to offer us as children by faith. However, sometimes we can miss them if we are not looking for God's work in our lives. Our eyes need to be focused on the good things going on around us, or we will miss seeing all the good happening. We can so easily be distracted by the bad things that we fail to see the good that God is doing for us. Again, renewing the mind means learning how to train your mind to focus on the glass being half full, not half empty.

God's perfect will for us never fails so we must remain on guard to always keep our hearts in line with His written word and the Holy Spirit. God is truth and He is love. By letting Him lead you and guide you, you can ultimately never go wrong. You will end up with copious amounts of indescribable, everlasting joy in Christ, despite whatever it is you may be facing! Seek the Lord first and everything else will fall into place in *His* perfect timing.

## Chapter 9

# Rejoice

*"Rejoice in the Lord always. I will say it*
*again: Rejoice!"* (Philippians 4:4)

Rejoice in the Lord always because He is so good to all of us, first and foremost because He simply chooses to love us despite all of our imperfections and flaws. He chooses to love us because He is love and only seeks to give us love. In the midst of the darkness when our lives seem to be carried by the deepest, darkest storms, we can rejoice because of His great love. We can rejoice because we are redeemed and re-born from heaven above as a whole new creation (see 2 Co 5:17).

Whenever you feel low and it seems nothing is going your way, remember all of the victories and things that He has already done for you. Sit in silence and dwell upon the fact that you are not going to hell because you have been saved by the blood of Jesus! Don't sit around and be miserable. Don't allow yourself to sink into your lonesome pit even further, rejoice! Rejoice because God is! God is with us all the time, everywhere. He feels our pains, yet His wisdom teaches us something through every situation. We can gain a great deal of wisdom and apply the knowledge He has given if we seek Him, have the desire to learn, and walk it out with Him. Push through the tough times and He will teach and restore you.

We can celebrate even in the midst of distress. Sounds like a crazy thought, but we can, because *Jesus* is our stability. Jesus keeps us stable and able to move forward with a good attitude and praises of acclamation to our King, our God. If you keep praising Him even in the midst of pain, He will provide the breakthrough at the right time. We are more than conquerors (Ro 8:37). We have victory everywhere we go, but we must choose to walk in it. We can choose the pit or we can choose God's way. God's way is the higher way, not a place of desolation and despair.

Jesus teaches us how to be more than conquerors if we trust and rely on His strength, not our own. If we only rely on ourselves, we will fail miserably to ever get out of the pit and live a fulfilling life of true, lasting happiness. No matter what you seek, first and foremost over everything it must be God. When we fail to keep our priorities straight, life becomes tangled like vines of atrocities and wickedness. The enemy has evil ways of slithering into our minds, our hearts, our actions, and our attitudes if we do not keep our eyes focused directly on God.

If your life feels a mess, ask yourself, "Where is my mind set?" What do you constantly think about? Is it worldly, earthly things that keep you stuck in the pit, or is your focus and mind set on seeking God amongst His prophetic ways? One cannot become all that he or she is called to be if his eyes are not kept directly on things above. We are taught by God's holy wisdom to set our minds and eyes on Him, and keep them set above, on heavenly ways and heavenly places (see Col 3:1-2). Our attitudes must revolve around God, and from there He helps us to go forth with everything else we need to do in life, whether that is to finish housework or go on a mission trip. We all have priorities and a life to live, but we must make God our first priority.

Stop and think who or what is first in your life? If God is not your first and number one priority *consistently* in your life, you have just found why things may not be lining up in your circumstances. If God is already first in your life on a consistent basis, congratulations! Remember to trust in Him, love Him with your whole heart, and seek His Word in scripture diligently to keep fulfilling His promise for you in the gift of your everyday life.

# Chapter 10

# Unity in Christ

When people come together as one instead of working against each other, something powerful happens to the inner self. We feel different, talk different, and act different because we get a sense of unity, a sense of enjoyment that only being one in Christ can bring. When we work together and join together, whether it is in free time or to get work done, so much more is accomplished and there is so much more room for enjoyment in the heart. Sounds like a simple concept we were taught in grade school, yet in the world today we see much more division than connection. People do things to hurt each other causing great harm, sometimes being aware of the pain caused and other times not. Many times we remark, "How could they do something like that" yet often, we don't take the time to wonder what deep down inside is causing them to act the way they do. There is a reason and a story behind every person's pain. Satan seeks to destroy and one of his main objectives is to turn people against each other. If we don't guard against it we can easily fall into his trap.

Behind every person, there is a life-long journey full of moments that created an individual's life. The biggest lesson is that hurting people will hurt and wound other people. Satan puts blinders on people so at times we do not see the reality of our actions. We can be deceived into lies of the enemy and so we must conform to God's ways to protect us from this indignation. We can get even or we can choose to let God be our vindication, as He promises. We are to overcome evil with good (Ro 12: 21), not repay wrong for wrong. This only opens the doorway for Satan to enter even further to cause greater damage. When there is injustice, there must also be a place for love to step in. Maybe it's not fair, but God doesn't promise life to be fair. He promises that if we are faithful to Him, He will make the injustices in our lives right. He promises to be our strength through the turmoil and our vindication. In our weakness He is strong (2 Co 12:9).

God tells us not to judge others critically because He is the only Judge. What we are judgmental and critical upon other people for, we ourselves could be blindly doing the same thing or worse without awareness of it (for study see Mt 7:1-6). This is why we are warned by God's word not to be critical of others and to let Him deal with our situations. This is a time when we must learn to trust Him to deal with our trials while we leave our hands off. This is going to require patience, adherence to the Word, and a steadfast mindset on God's truth.

Giving and showing love, while it may not seem fair, can win hearts of stone to Christ. His love shown through us towards other hurting people can be the reason someone softens and opens up their life to Christ. The redemption of people is more important than acting in the flesh and pleasing our souls by getting even out of hostility. Our souls want vengeance; our spirit wants the peace and love of God to prevail. We must key in to differentiate between the two. Choose to walk in the Spirit and not the flesh, and resist temptation to fall into the trap of judging critically what others are doing without truly knowing what is or has gone on in their personal life. Love must come first. Love must be the action we show first if we are going to claim to be Christians and followers of Jesus Christ. Recall the old, yet familiar adage, WWJD– What Would Jesus Do. Reflect on Christ, study what He would do, and walk in His footsteps of love.

# Chapter 11

# Don't Quit

It can be said that every person has a destiny, a life to fulfill. The question is then, "are you following it?" Maybe you're reading this and thinking you have no idea what your purpose is; and that's okay. For many of us, we struggle to find our "place". We are unsure of why we are here and even where to begin on this journey called life. One thing is certain and that is your future is great. Wherever you are right now, if you push through, there is more greatness, more opportunity, and more fulfilment lying ahead of you. At times we get stuck, not moving forward because we feel afraid, unsure, or have no idea where to step next. Remember that the Lord guides our steps, so no matter which step you take, if you trust Him, He will guide you where and when to move. We cannot let fear stop us from taking chances to reach our goals and our dreams. They are within us because we were innately given a place within our spirits to achieve great things. As we become more familiar with God's goodness, we can relax and let Him work in us to guide us in the direction we are called to go.

If we step out and choose the wrong path, it is not meant to stop us and cause us to give up. We can learn something from it, receive greater empowerment from God, and try again. I once was taught by a great and inspirational leader, "The only way to fail is to quit." When you live knowing God's Spirit lives inside of you, you know quitting is not an option. You know whatever you are facing will be conquered and lead you to your greatest destiny because it is God that makes it happen, not ourselves. We partner with Him. When we learn to keep our minds set on our goals, personal dreams, and passions, holding them deeply in our hearts, we learn how to be focused. We learn how to zone in on our God-given potential and use it to live a life to achieve whatever we are meant to do.

We each have our unique paths, so we must be careful not to follow too closely to what someone else is doing. We are to learn from others, but not mimic someone else's life. God creates this space in our brains to dream, have a vision, and be unstoppable, but we must learn how to tap into that creativity. With His help and learning how to be led by His Spirit, it may take months, years, or a lifetime, but we can reach exactly what our destination is for this life.

Don't stress about being perfect or making mistakes. Relax in God's perfection, knowing that we are flawless in God's eyes because He sent His everlasting Son to die for us. Through Him, we are already perfected and we can concentrate on living a life that pleases Him, one day at a time. He leads, He guides, and He promises to never leave us. Seek His guidance, that gentle knowing in your heart, by continual prayer (consistent conversation) to let Him lead the way to your mission. We all have one and we are all unique, but are of one body in Christ so we can all work together to create unity by our individual purposes. When we take the focus off of self, money, possessions, and fame, we can relax in our struggles and focus on Him, knowing we are on a journey and we will end up filling the right shoes, sitting exactly where we are supposed to be, at the right time.

## Chapter 12

# Peace Be With You

We all start in a place of complacency, a place where we feel there's more to be had. Yet at times, even though things don't change we can find a great sense of peace, a great sense of joy, and a great sense of abundance that comes by looking to Jesus when we are choosing to follow Him. He offers the life of abundance we all seek to naturally find and crave. This abundant life given is freely offered as His gift because of His true sacrifice for us. The abundance comes when we find it through God. Let's review. Jesus says, *"Peace I leave with you; My [own] peace I now give and bequeath to you. Not as the world gives do I give to you. Do not let your hearts be troubled, neither let them be afraid. [Stop allowing yourselves to be agitated and disturbed; and do not permit yourselves to be fearful and intimidated and cowardly and unsettled]."* (Jn 14:27 AMP) He clearly reminds us He does not give in the same way the world offers abundance and gifts to us. He is the Giver of life, so we can rise up from the death we feel in our souls, and live the life of peace and joy only Jesus has to give.

When we rise up on the inside and decide to take hold of that special gift, that special type of life that can only be found by seeking Jesus, nothing can get in our way of happiness; neither trials, nor troubles. We can have this unstoppable spirit of joy when we keep our eyes and focus on Jesus. He is the giver and keeper of peace. He ordains peace in our lives if we choose to go after it. By seeking His ways instead of what this world offers, we can have something the rest of the world doesn't have. We can have a life of serenity and extreme gladness. Why? Not because our lives are perfect and without pain, but because Jesus DIED to give every single one of us this great life.

So why does it seem that some have this life of joy and others don't? One thing that greatly affects the way we live is our attitude and mindset. When you put God first and focus on His goodness you will find inner joy. When you focus on the world, your troubles and your hardships, this joy will be missing. Your attitude must stay lined up with the way God thinks, and God is good. Don't keep your mind set on the darkness of the pit, but keep it set that God works all things out for good if we trust Him (Ro 8:28). No matter how bad things seem, God never loses control. If you keep your mind and attitude in praise on Him and His goodness, He can take every situation, turn it for good, and give you the life you can dare to dream.

This, of course, requires godly trust, patience, and character; not a human, fleshly trust, patience, and character. It requires keeping a good attitude right in the middle of the storm. It requires not giving up and seeking His peace. He offers things we cannot ever get from our own effort or from the world. We can't achieve peace without God. We can't achieve joy, happiness, wisdom, strength, or any of the qualities we crave for a great and abundant life.

God desires for us to be greatly blessed and sometimes this is having nice things, but His greatest priority is this life of abundance Jesus offers; the renewed qualities Jesus offers deep within our souls that we long for. At times, our flesh (our own minds), will think that if we have possessions those things will make us happy, but when we focus on Jesus we quickly find possessions or people will not give us the abundance or happiness Jesus speaks of in His Word. Jesus has and is everything we need. We can feel fulfilled and live the abundant life when we choose Jesus instead of chasing after people's approval, possessions, money, fame, or the like. Jesus will solve all that we seek to fix by ourselves. Jesus is always the only pathway to the fulfillment of the abundant life of true, lasting peace every one of us can have.

# Chapter 13

# The All Sufficient One

J esus promises that if we come to Him He will always take care of us and protect us. God never will leave us or forsake us, nor leave us for harm (Dt 31:6). We can rest in knowing that He is "Jehovah-Jireh" (Yahweh-Yireh), the Lord our Provider (for biblical study see Genesis 22). We can rely on Him to fully take care of us, so long as we fully put our trust in Him. We cannot waiver in our faith and be inconsistent, one day trusting Him, the next day having a lack of trust. We are called to know Him deeply in such a way that we never doubt that He is good and know that He will never leave us. We can have a special assurance in our hearts that nothing else can provide. Truly knowing Jesus brings ease to our souls and comfort to our hearts. We can never deny His goodness when we look for it all around us. I challenge you to start looking for His goodness all around you.

You've heard the verbiage of the glass being half full or seeing it half empty. Try seeing things on the upscale and look to what you do have rather than what you don't have. This brings a deeper satisfaction and a greater reliance on Him, knowing that He is taking care of us daily. God is our provider. What we can sometimes fail to see is that without Him, we would not even be here. He is the One who gave birth to our being. He is the

Creator and the Finisher. We must not fail to overlook God's goodness, and instead focus on what we may lack.

To be rich and prosperous simply means that we have Jesus Christ and He has us. There are no riches greater than this. When we can acknowledge that those of us who are lucky enough to know the Lord and are going to heaven, we fully understand that we are the richest people in all of creation. A right heart combined with a right love seeks one thing, and that is to fully grasp the intimacy and relationship with our Lord Jesus Christ. He is and always will be, and I encourage you to get busy telling someone else about the love of God.

What are you doing to help someone else? This shows Jesus' love and character. This allows us to be witness to His all sufficient love to others because He is providing to them through us. This may be achieved through encouraging words or a warm meal provided to a stranger in need, or your neighbor next door. Who are you blessing with the love of Jesus Christ that you too have been blessed with? It is by action we share the Gospel of Christ. It isn't by passivity that we are members of His love. He calls us to go out into the world and to do good to those who are in need. A helping hand and a loving heart can win a lost soul to Jesus Christ, providing them with the gift of eternity.

When we go out into the world and truly act like the disciples of Jesus, as we are called to be, we can be the shining light in the dark places and the salt that makes people thirsty for more, thirsty to know why we chose to love when in this world we are surrounded by much hate. For one person, we could be a blessing and the answer for their heartache because we have been so inclined by the touch of God's hand in our own life. We can provide the answer to the way to Life: Jesus Christ. Because Jesus is all sufficient for us, we can go out and be all sufficient to someone else and create a domino effect of blessings and salvation. What better way to open the door to a conversation about the Answer you know that they need! Be bold and be an answer for someone else.

# Chapter 14

# The Love Journey

By sowing and planting good seeds into another's life we can reap the reward of knowing the true gift of giving. Jesus reminds us that *"it is more blessed to give than to receive"* (Ac 20:35). We can experience His divine words of wisdom when we follow the Holy Spirit leading us to go out of our way to be good to others. A good rule of thumb to follow is if you are hurting, help someone else. This opens the door for someone else to become a blessing to you also. God is merciful to provide His love, and He works through all of us. We can experience a different type of joy if we take our minds off ourselves and begin to focus on helping those around us who are hurting. In return, our load becomes lighter because we are filled with happiness knowing that we planted a seed of goodness in someone else's life. A simple act of kindness can seem small to us, but a large blessing of hope to someone else.

As humans we have the ability to hide our painful feelings. When we take the opportunity to be a blessing to someone else, it may impact their life at a time when they most desperately need it on the inside. It shows them someone cares, and many people are living a life of loneliness feeling that everyone has forgotten them. Most of us can say we have experienced this at some point in our lives. When we take the initiative to step out and be a blessing, God sees it, and He will honor it. He sees our hearts and is pleased when we follow His ways of wisdom. This shows character and is a beautiful witness to the love of Jesus Christ.

Jesus told Peter to follow Him and be a fisher of people (Mt 4:19). We can see by this proclamation to Peter and later, the rest of His disciples, that together they would change the world. By working together with Jesus, we too can help to make a difference in this world. We can work for God daily, by seeking people to be good to. It is not simply everyone else's job to do; it is our responsibility to be one who can help make a difference, whether that is in one person at a time or ten thousand. When God leads by His Spirit, we are to follow. When we do our best to seek God's guidance, He will provide the way. He will show us where to move forward and what to do. We must be open to let Him lead us and not be shut down for fear that it will require work on our part. What He asks us to do we can do, as long as we stay in step with Him. His plan will be fulfilled perfectly if we are doing His will by walking His walk, not following our own fleshly path that focuses on self.

When we remember we are not here for ourselves but rather we are here for Him, we become open vessels for Him to work. We become a living, breathing testimony of the love of God. Where He takes us, we won't always know, but we will be safe right in His loving arms to go forward and carry out His will. You may feel uneasy knowing that God could ask us to partake in the unknown, but let me remind you that this is faith. Our journey is always a walk by faith, and we are not to worry, rather listen. We are to perform His will. Imagine not yet knowing the love of Christ and that you have never heard about His redemption of sins. Imagine not knowing that we are forever saved and can live in heaven for all eternity. Would you want someone to tell you about Him? Yes! The alternative is an eternity in a place called hell, a place of eternal torture (see Rev 20:10), and eternal separation from God (see Rev 20:14-15). This is why we must not hold back in sharing and doing.

If you have ever been in a place in your life where you have been in a pit, a place of brokenness and pain, you know you need the love of Christ to pull you out, and sometimes this is simply by a friend who cares. We need to be active in our walk with God and share His love with those we meet. It is a progressive journey, not a lackadaisical stroll. When we are active to be part of God's work, we will see blessings unto ourselves pop up unexpectedly because God is good, and He loves to bless His children!

# Chapter 15

# Action

Complacency and passivity are not the work of God. He encourages us to be bold and fearless because His perfect love casts out fear. This doesn't mean we will never fear what lies ahead but we can move forward, confident in the fact that God has got our backs if we trust Him. He is no respecter of persons and He loves us all the same (Ac 10:34 KJV), so He will lift up every single one of us when we fall back in defeat; we are not to allow ourselves to stay in a place of defeat. We are to move boldly and confidently ahead to fulfill Jesus' personal touch in our life. We must trust Him to take care of us as we move forward in the places we are called to pursue. When we follow God's lead, we can always be sure we are headed down the right path. We may not always clearly see it or understand, but we can rest easy and know we are lifted up by His protective hand.

We see God's provision by His amazing grace. We cannot save ourselves, yet we have a great amount of other work to fulfill for the Lord's path for us. We are not to get focused on ourselves, although sometimes we start out that way. We are to focus on Him and His provisions. Many times we can't see His way ahead of time, but it is only in hindsight that we understand. True faith boldly marches forward by trusting and not always knowing the next step. It is in our intimate relationship with our Father we can start to discern His given will for us. We can also know when (yet maybe not why) to take a step.

True faith cannot always see the way, but it knows God is in control and He will never forsake us. He is the One we can always lean on and count on when all else has failed around us. He reaches down, lifts us up, and sets us upright. When we reciprocate His action and grab onto His hand, we know we are unstoppable. No matter how bleak the circumstance, we push through until we see a clearing in the pathway. We keep pushing until we hit our breakthrough. Our personal breakthroughs come with faith, trust, and persistence. We cannot doubt or take our focus off our Leader, God Himself, as number one. This is critical to remember; we are to follow one person alone and that is God, manifested to us through Jesus Christ and His Holy Spirit. The eternal three in One is always with us. Confusing as it can be, God is Jesus, and God is also the Holy Spirit. He reveals Himself to us in three persons, or three different, yet similar ways. He will work so intimately with each one of us until we fully grasp His love for us and how deep His divine love is. We can't ever humanly grasp this full agape love of God, but He continually reveals it, as we continually seek Him. God is forever and delights in the fact that His saved children will live with Him forever, even after we leave this earth.

Maybe you are feeling like you have lost that closeness with Him somewhere along the line. I encourage you to step up and seek Him fully, continually, and diligently. He never leaves us, but sometimes it can seem as though He is not present. Remember that He is always with you, and continue to go to Him day after day, never resting until you reignite that intimacy. Every one of us has a different relationship with the Lord, but He loves us all the same. When you diligently seek God, it shows that you honor and revere Him above all else and it will only be a matter of time until you regain that closeness. Don't give up. Pursue Him at all times and be completely open to hearing Him. Let Him pull you back in.

He is always with us (see Dt 31:8), but at times we may go through trials as so to seem we are tested in continuing to believe that He is still with us even if we don't see hear, or feel His presence. He is there. Be persistent in your craving of an intimate relationship with Him, never give up, and you will find a lasting relationship with Him that is more fulfilling than you could ever dream!

# Chapter 16

# Called to Love

We are called to love. First over anything else, we are to love God and then to love our neighbor, which means those we come in contact with. Emotions and feelings can rise up and try to overtake us, so loving can be challenging at times. First Corinthians 13 is a scripture teaching us of true love. We are taught that love is not a feeling, but a way of discipleship of Christ. By following His example, we can purposely choose to act in love towards other people. We are reminded throughout the Bible that we must do our best by following Jesus to love everyone, not just those who are friendly and kind to us. When we step into this love character, we become a true example of humility and shining light of Jesus Christ. We can't claim to be a genuine follower of Christ, and then act unkind or unloving to others. To walk in true Christ-like love, we must choose to put our feelings of fleshly ways aside, and choose to take up our own cross, as Jesus asked those to do who desire to be His true followers (Mt 16:24). We must become who He desires us to be through His help.

It is easy to claim to be witnesses of Jesus Christ, but are we acting humbly out of love on a consistent basis? Are we putting our own personal wants and needs to the side so we may intentionally serve with a right heart? We can't have a right heart without Jesus being the Lord over our whole life, not just pieces of it. As we choose to put Jesus first instead of ourselves, He shows us how to act. He teaches us His ways, and we need to follow, which means we accept His guidance and obey. Here at this crossing point, we can pretend we didn't hear Him and ignore what we know deep down is right, or we can choose Jesus Christ. When we put Him first, everything in our own lives will become beautiful and genuine as we choose to walk with Him. This is a steadfast journey, not a fast paced sprint. We are called to walk it out, to walk out the life He has set before us where we learn, grow, and mature to become more like Him and grow deeper in faith.

When we accept Jesus as our own personal Savior, we are submitting to Him as the Lord of our lives; our entire lives, not just the parts we choose to give to Him. He sets Himself before us so that we follow Him and revere Him in love. We get to choose if we submit or rebel to His ways. He does not tell us anything simply because He has power. He shows us how to live so that we can have the great life He desires for us to have. If we pray, listen, obey, and follow, we will without a doubt have the most amazing life. If we will walk it out, step by step, and let Him lead, we will find our divine purpose. This means we keep our eyes on Him and let Him be the Leader. At this place, we put our own thoughts and desires to the side and chose to seek His ways first.

In doing this, we will be taught how to love with a right heart, not by feelings. We will be taught a life of greatness, integrity, and wisdom. On our journey, as we submit and desire to please Him first, He will reward us because He loves us, not because we are "good". We are saved and He loves us not because of the good actions we perform, but because He is good and He chose us as He died on the cross. He chose to love us first so we could have a wonderful life. We don't have to be perfect because He Himself is perfect and makes us perfect in His sight (see Col 1:22-23). His perfection allows us to relax and simply try our best. God watches and scans the earth, and He sees every single one of us at all times. He knows our hearts and our inner desire to please Him. He is not distant and angry at you, but the complete expression of love (see 1 Jn 4:16). He seeks to love and be good to us, but He also expects us to love Him because He first loved us. He doesn't ever expect us to be perfect.

God is revealed to us by the closeness of Jesus Christ in our hearts. When Jesus is our life, God becomes our life and our desires change. We now have an everlasting desire to serve and love Him out of reverence for God. Therefore, because we have the gift of knowing Jesus intimately, we also have the gift of receiving the Holy Spirit, so we can have the power to make all of these things work together. Sometimes things will be logical and make sense if you follow God's promptings, but sometimes they won't. It's not up to us to decide if it makes sense to us. It's up to us to decide if we will listen and obey. We cannot listen and run away from what we hear if we want intimacy, a real closeness with God. It is in running away that we will only push Him further away in our lives. He does not make Himself distant. We sometimes cause the distance, and God does allow us to go through these testing times.

If a time comes we must be in the wilderness where it feels we are left on our own, it is a time to prove our faithfulness to God. It is a time that means no matter what we go through we trust Him fully with submissive patience and reverence. We still seek Him and go after Him with all our might, but we rely on this faithfulness and promise to us that He will never leave us. God is a person of integrity and true, unwavering faithfulness who will never depart from His children. Ask yourself today, am I seeking God first in my life *every day*?

# Chapter 17

# Jesus is The Answer

To share in the glory of Jesus also means we must share in His sufferings. This can be scary and somewhat overwhelming at times, but we are not to fear because God is in control. Anything we go through we can come out stronger because we can trust in Jesus' strength to never fail us. We need not look at our own strength or we will fall. We can look to Him to bring us glory in the midst of every circumstance and trust that He is always present with His unfailing love. Suffering in this life is bound to happen but as we walk those trials, we can pull closer to Him and really get to know Him. Some choose to pull away but God's wisdom says move closer. Godly wisdom says seek to grow closer to our Provider, our Shield, and our Protector. He is always in the midst of us and we can rejoice because God is good, all the time. His goodness never fails; He never fails. He is faithful and loyal to those who put their entire trust in Him and learn to rely on Him constantly. When we truly seek Him by thought, word, and deed in prayer, we will always find Him.

Jesus teaches us not to be afraid in this life because He wants us to understand that God is our protective covering and He cannot fail. When we trust, He works. When we ask Him with a right heart to go to work for us, He answers, although we may not always see it right away. So many times we get the enjoyment of watching Him work in our lives on our behalf. He will always be the lifter of our head to guide us and lead us on the path we need to take. At times, we will make mistakes, but we trust and learn to get back up. We all can relate to each other because we have one main purpose and that is we are here for God. He created us and we were made to follow Him. When we learn to diligently seek our Creator, we will find His love and goodness.

He always helps us on our path to what we can call "life". He leads us to a place of divine destiny that is filled with a heart of joy and gratitude towards our Creator. We can learn to be grateful when everything else around us is falling apart. We can choose to have His attitude of greatness instead of despair. It is a choice and many times not an easy one, but through Christ we can choose God's attitude because in Him we have the greatest strength we will ever need.

Christ suffered so we could rejoice in all circumstances, every single day of our lives, to worship Him and revere Him as our Lord and Savior. He suffered and died so we could be joyful and know what true happiness feels like. He offers this one thing that nothing else can buy or bring into our lives. He died and shed His blood for you, because He loves; because He loves you. From our human mind standpoint, we can't make sense of this. Yet, as we study God's word, scripture is ultimately clear this is the Truth. Jesus can become our truth if we learn to seek Him and follow Him.

Maybe you have gone to church all your life, but the reality of what Jesus did for you and who He is, was never fully grasped? Jesus is the answer to a life of inner joy. Jesus is the answer to a bleeding heart recovered into healing. Jesus is the answer to every problem, care, or concern you are facing, and ever will face. He is the Answer. Whatever else you chase, seek, or try to find, will never be the lasting, fulfilling answer you seek. Until you willfully understand accepting Christ as the ultimate answer to everything you desire is the only way to true joy and happiness, there will always we one thing, something, you lack. Completeness can't happen except by a life with Jesus Christ. Going to church won't make that happen. Doing good deeds won't make that happen. Living a life filled with Jesus Christ is the only way to a refreshing, redeeming, life of complete happiness, joy, and abundance. All the rest will continue to leave you hopeless, with no chance at lasting, true, finality of success in all of life. Keep your eyes and heart focused on one thing; the Savior, and you will start to feel a true joy your heart has never understood before. Jesus said, *"I am the way and the truth and the life"* (Jn 14:6).

# Chapter 18

# Celebrate

Because Christ was sent and came to earth as man, we can celebrate each day of our lives. Every day is a gift, a blessing to be cherished. It has been given to us to freely live a life of joy. Circumstances can bring us down, and even our mind can bring us down, but we don't need to let that affect our daily walk with the Lord. With Jesus, every day can be a celebration. Every day can be filled with the true joy of being saved and knowing that we are going to heaven. At times our emotions can persuade us otherwise. Earthly feelings can make us feel like we are on a roller-coaster of ups and downs because life seems to be up and down, but we don't need to allow those feelings to control us. We can live with full assurance that because Jesus reigns, we have reason to celebrate!

Jesus came so we could be free. He has come so we don't need to live bogged down by the weight of life. He connects with us so we can rely on Him every day to keep a true smile on our faces because we are free and free to be happy no matter what life throws at us. Each moment that passes is a moment we can never get back. Don't waste your life looking back and thinking you wish you would have chosen to keep a right attitude and live the happiness Jesus died for you to have. Don't look back thinking, "I wish." It's there for the taking, we just need to learn to tap into the strength and power of Jesus Christ and not let the enemy run all over us because we feel weak.

We are not weak, we are one with God, and we have the right as His children to walk in His love and freedom because Jesus died for that. Jesus died so we can live, not just an eternal life in heaven, but an extreme life of fulfillment here on earth. Maybe you are in a pit right now that seems so unbearable, you don't see how this could be possible for you, but it is. Jesus gives His strength to us to use. We must seek to be closer to Jesus and we will find the strength we need. It takes time and patience, but as you begin to think like Jesus, the way God chooses for us to think, we can align our thoughts with the Creator's. In time, our mind, and our heart will begin to see a new life filled with the peace and love of God. He allows us to have such a close connection with Him because He does not wish for us to be miserable. He chooses an abundance of happiness in heart, mind, spirit, and soul, but we must learn to walk with Him.

We can't speak from our mouths and think in our minds the opposite of the way God speaks in His written Word and how He thinks of us. We are divinely created with His love and compassion. We must be careful not to take on an ungrateful attitude which comes from the heavy burden of the enemy. Our lives can sometimes be seen as a battle of good versus evil; God verses the enemy. As we begin to view God as our powerhouse, where all our inner strength and being comes from, our real selves begin to shine forth. Grab onto God and He will grab onto you. He waits for us to call intimately for His help and when we do, He begins to work. It is crucial that at this time we remain an open-minded vessel for Him to use to download His virtues and teach us about Him. We have to learn to listen. We have to learn to put Him first so that He can show us what we are blindly missing in our own earthly knowledge. He gives when we are ready and willing to listen and stop giving excuses. If you are ready for His change to lift you up in your own life, desire God first by giving Him your heart and your full attention. Slowly, but surely, you will be exalted.

# Chapter 19

# The Redeemer

By now, it's possible you may be starting to wonder, why am I really here; what's my main purpose on this earth? Others, after reading, are hopefully reassured and know exactly their path. The one common purpose among all of us is that we were all put here for one divine reason first and foremost, and that is to love and serve God with our whole heart by accepting His Son, our personal Savior Jesus Christ. We can't figure out our lives without Him being in first place. God lovingly reminds us in His word that we can do nothing apart from Him (Jn 15:5). When we continue to separate ourselves from Him even in the slightest way and try to figure everything out while we run our own life, we will not make true, lasting progress with happiness. This won't happen until we choose to submit to His guidance and put Jesus first. We can save a lot of time from being wasted if we choose His power over our own.

We can easily forget God has everything already planned out and He can see what's before us. Doesn't it make logical sense to follow our Leader who can already see ahead of us? Things will become much easier and more flowing when we learn to be led by God and obey promptly. When He speaks through His promptings, the Word, His voice, or through other people, we need to listen. He walks before us guiding our every breath and our every move. We cannot be or exist without God. He must become your life. Only then, will your gift of life continue to get better and better. Life will be so pleasing to us that we begin to wonder how we ever got to that place. *"Let us not become weary in doing good, for at the proper time we will reap a harvest if we do not give up"* (Gal 6:9).

Our goal must be to push forward and to not give up. God is our partner. With Him, we will never ultimately fail. We may have setbacks and obstacles, things that don't work out, but we learn and keep pushing through. We don't quit and we run at life full force forward with an attitude of gratitude, and God is right beside us laying out the foundation. He already has our success and happiness planned out. He already knows the mistakes we'll make and the different roads we'll travel. God is not surprised by us or by our actions. He chooses to love and teach us the way in which we should go. He is clear and specific if we let Him lead and we follow.

Let us remember playing the children's game of "Simon says". Our child-like relationship with God should be similar. He speaks; we listen carefully to the instructions, and do only what the leader says, with clear-cut directions. We learn as we go; we listen for His voice. We ask for His wisdom with guidance and He provides. With God, it is not luck of the draw. He purposely chooses all of us, not just those who are lucky enough to know Him. As our Heavenly Father He hand-picked all of us. He is near, not far. He is close to our heart. We can call on Him and find Him whenever we need. He is perfect in all of His ways and is the complete expression of love. He cannot hate any one of us because God is love.

Sometimes we try to follow God and try to learn, but we don't know where to start. A great place to start in studying is "love". Take the time to learn what God's love means, feels, and looks like. Begin to apply it in your own life. Study it. Meditate on it by reading about His love over and over again until it takes root. It will teach you a great deal about God's character and who He genuinely is along with how He feels about us as His prized children. He doesn't ever reject any of His children. We have the pleasure and privilege to be with Him, and to call on Him, day and night. Seek to be close to Him and He will be close to you. Stop seeking things in this world to fulfill your place of happiness. Temporary happiness can be found by things; everlasting happiness can only be found with God.

Jesus is the Savior who saves. He is the great Redeemer. He watches over us and never lets us go. We are redeemed, *"with the precious blood of Christ, a lamb without blemish or defect"* (1 Pe 1:19). Each day is a precious gift from God and is to be seen that way. We function, live, breathe, and have every movement because of our Lord God. Every breath is a gift that should not be taken for granted. God tells us we are the apple of His eye, and He cannot be mocked. If we fully believe in Him and His Son, we are saved by His grace and He is there in heart, mind, and soul. Not a second goes by that He is not with you, and He takes delight in each of us. Where else can we find that? Nowhere! We are exceptional, beautiful, and blameless in His sight. We need not fear because He is with us wherever we go.

What is holding you back in life? What is stopping you from reaching further? Reach into that place in your heart. Go at it and conquer it with God's strength. Don't be held back another single moment by letting the world hold you back. We are meant to be dreamers and achievers. We aren't meant to sit back and be happy with just getting by, just getting through another day to say we made it. God gave us the ability to dream and to always come up higher. We are innately made to reach for more. We are created uniquely and delicately to be different, yet the same in Christ. Reach to achieve the passions within you. You're never too late, too old, or too young to dream. Ignite the passions within you, the fire inside you, and watch God work.

Seek His counsel and His plans first, and He will always guide you. He will guide you into your own personal truth, prosperity, and everlasting peace with great happiness. No one can stop His plan for you, but be careful you don't stop yourself. You are beautiful inside and out because God made you that way. Stop looking at what you didn't do or how things look impossible. Go after what God tells you *is* possible. Remember that He sees what you cannot. He will never lead you down a broken path to failure or guide you into a life of wounds. He is a protective Shield to surround you and a Comforter to hold on to.

Man cannot thwart God's intentional purpose for you (Job 42:2). Reach out to Him and go after whatever He has placed in your heart; don't fight it. Be a child again and dream your way into greatness. Allow your visions to take flight and let them soar to your God-given destiny. "Quitters never win and winners never quit." In God's eyes, He sees us the same. We are not losers, or quitters, and we have a purpose. We are the raised up, perfected children of the Most High God; don't be afraid to say it. Look to Him and He will give you the desires of your heart. Don't look to people, things, or success, but look to God and He will help to create whatever it is you are reaching for. Follow His path, His guidance, and His ways of wisdom and there will be no stopping you. Take delight in Him and He will provide your lasting joy. Go to Him like never before and act as though you are desperate for the first time.

Maybe this is the first time in your life you have been truly desperate for God. Today is a fresh, new day. Go to Him with expectancy, with a renewed, fresh heart full of desire. He will start with you wherever you are. Don't be afraid of Him or pull away, for when you seek to be near Him, He delights in your desire, and He will move closer to you. Love Him with an open mind and open heart, and watch Him be the greatness you desire! Seek the Kingdom of God above all else, and everything else shall be added unto you (see Mt 6:33).

God will always know you better than you know yourself. Whenever you feel alone or afraid, He is there. Whenever you are desperate or in pain, He is there. These are the times you must go to Him and don't shy away from His love. He's waiting for every one of us to relinquish our own control and follow Him. When you decide to fully give Him your life, He can start to do exceedingly above and beyond all that you dare dream, ask, or imagine (see Jn 10:10). Put God first and watch Him be the great Redeemer of your entire life!

*"But those who wait for The Lord (who expect, look for, and hope in Him) shall change and renew their strength and power; they shall lift their wings and mount up (close to God) as eagles (mount up to the sun); they shall run and not be weary, they shall walk and not faint or become tired."* (Isaiah 40:31 AMP)

# About the Author

Kristy lives in Pennsylvania and works as a certified personal trainer, wellness coach, and the owner of Kickstart Fitness for Women. *Everlasting Life* is the result of a personal encounter with the Lord and His love, calling her into ministry, and the creation of Shackles Ministries. Shackles Ministries foundational mission is bringing people to salvation and setting people free from bondage through the healing power of Jesus Christ.